HOW I STEAL FROM YOU
THEFT WITHIN THE HOSPITALITY INDUSTRY

CHLOE RACHEL HOWARD

JAUNA L WERNER

Copyright © 2025 Unfiltered Ink Media, LLC

All rights reserved. This work may not be translated or copied in whole or in part without the written permission of the authors except for brief excerpts in connection with reviews, news articles or scholarly analysis. Use in connection with any form of information storage and retrieval, electronic adaptation, computer software including artificial intelligence, or by similar or dissimilar methodology not known or hereafter developed is forbidden without written permission from the Publisher.

This publication is designed to provide accurate and authoritative information in regard to the subject matter covered at the time of publication. It is sold on the understanding that the Publisher is not engaged in rendering professional services. If professional advice or other expert assistance is required regarding any subject matter covered in this book, the services of a competent professional should be sought.

Unfiltered Ink Media, LLC books may be purchased for educational, business, or sales promotional use. For information, please email: info@unfilteredinkmedia.com

ISBN eBook- 979-8-9940123-2-1

Cover Design and Illustrations: Allart Jensen

❀ Formatted with Vellum

the MENU

STARTERS
CHAPTER 1 – why?
CHAPTER 2 – a day in the life
CHAPTER 3 – setting the table

ENTREES
CHAPTER 4 – crooked clockers
CHAPTER 5 – inventory infiltrators
CHAPTER 6 – the snake
CHAPTER 7 – cash stashers
CHAPTER 8 – frequent fraudsters
CHAPTER 9 – villainous vendors
CHAPTER 10 – shady customers

DESSERTS
CHAPTER 11 – oh, the humanity
CHAPTER 12 – last call

All parties are subject to 100% cited sources upon book completion.

CHAPTER 1
WHY?

People find joy in different ways. For some, it's a long walk on the beach or a relaxing vacation. People enjoy scrapbooking and bingo; some people love to hit the casinos, while others like to curl up on the couch and knit a blanket. Many people derive joy from going to see a movie or going bowling, and some love nothing more than a hot bowl of chili and a football game on a Sunday afternoon.

The authors of this book like to eat. Specifically, we like to eat out at restaurants, and often, we choose an independent mom-and-pop venue. We also have our favorite "chain" brands when we are looking for comfort food or are on the road.

There is an unbridled joy that comes from the experience of scanning the menu, reading the descriptions, seeing the various plates delivered to our neighboring tables and interrogating the servers about the best things to try. Making our selection is often a hard decision, as if it is our last meal and we will never eat again. We like to exchange bites from our respective plates and take pictures of the food before feasting.

Every aspect of the meal is exquisite for us, from the first cocktail to the last bite of dessert and accompanying espresso, *if available*. We like to learn the stories of the restaurants, how they came to be, how long they've been there, and we love to meet the owners. We marvel at the artistic presentation of the food we are consuming. Like the Siskel and Ebert of the hospitality industry, we exchange commentary on every single bite. We take in the entire experience and share a peaceful and satisfying sense of completion when the restaurant delivers the goods.

Dining out is our indulgence and guilty pleasure, but without the guilt. There is a genuine joy found for us in supporting a small business owner, in knowing that the food is prepared with love and care, and in knowing that we are helping restaurant owners and staff fulfill their dreams of providing outstanding food and service.

Unfortunately, many of our beloved restaurants are struggling. The cost of goods is higher than ever. It is difficult to find reliable staff. Consumers are fighting to make ends meet, and when it's time to trim the fat, the first piece that gets cut from the budget is often dining out. To stay in business, restaurants may compromise the quality of goods, the shelf life of their products and their staff headcounts, which ultimately affects the overall guest experience negatively. With over 90% of consumers choosing where they are going to eat based on online reviews, a couple of bad guest experiences can spell certain doom for a restaurant in today's marketplace.

As two of the biggest fans of restaurants, we felt a call to action. Besides dining out, another bond that we share is finding tremendous joy in helping other people. We have spent our respective careers helping business owners thrive. For us, the mission of saving restaurants from being victimized by theft and potentially going out of business is a no-brainer. We have combined our love of restaurants with our desire to do good work in the world, and the book you're holding in your hand is the result.

In this chapter, we're going to give you a little backstory on where we both came from and why the topic of theft in the hospitality industry is so important to us. We are very different people with unique life experiences, but one of our common bonds is that we are good at solving problems, and as you will quickly see as you continue reading this book, there is a problem here to solve. There is no shortage of literature available for business owners on how to fine-tune their operations, and yet there is very little information available for hospitality owners covering the topic of theft within their businesses. It seems to be the elephant in the room that NOBODY is talking about… until now.

Chloe's Story

The first villainous story I remember hearing was about someone "stealing" from our family restaurant. We called it the "Story of the Robbers." In the early seventies, actual robbers followed my grandfather home on Valentine's Day after the restaurant closed. They were expecting him to have a bank bag full of cash for a deposit the next day. The robbers tied up my grandfather and his family and held them hostage in a home invasion.

Unbeknownst to the thieves, just a few days before, my grandfather had invested in a safe for the restaurant. He knew that bringing the cash home every night was risky. So, much to the disappointment of the robbers, on the night of their heist, there was no bank bag to be had. Fortunately, my grandfather had the foresight to realize that as a successful business owner, he would likely one day be a target of criminal mischief and theft. He followed his gut instincts and put a safeguard in place to protect the cash.

As a child, I grew up hearing the "Story of the Robbers" and how they held my family hostage. I always envisioned them in masks with guns. I have no idea what the actual robbers were wearing or what they looked like, but in my mind, clearly the stereotypical "robber villain" persona, like you would see in the cartoons. It never crossed my mind that a "robber" would look just like the rest of us or even look like a friend!

Many years later, our family restaurant was a booming business in our small town. I remember riding with my grandfather to the restaurant on Friday and Saturday nights so that he could drive through the parking lot and "count cars." It wasn't uncommon for us to pull up on those nights and see people lined up outside and around the building, waiting hours to get a table. The food was THAT good! Sometimes my grandfather would do his drive-by routine TWICE in one night, always filled with excitement while he counted cars and profits in his head as we cruised. The restaurant was truly our pride and joy. Life was good.

Years went by, and most days, when I got out of school, I walked to the restaurant and visited with the staff before I made my way home. Our family spent every holiday season celebrating with the people who worked at our restaurant. We enjoyed potlucks and get-togethers, and all the people were like family to me. I referred to all of them as "aunts" and "uncles" and adopted all of their families as my own extended tribe. The restaurant was my home-away-from-home and my safe place.

I imagined that one day I would marry and raise my own children in that same restaurant. They would learn how to make our famous recipes and how to greet guests. My children would one day be the face of the business and our family's legacy.

Everyone in town had a tab at our bar. If you were friends with us, you rarely paid. If you worked at the restaurant, you helped yourself to food whenever you were hungry. If we needed money for unexpected repairs, we simply collected cash and didn't ring the sales up. If we forgot to clock in, we wrote a time down on our time card and moved on. There was nowhere to track comps or spills. When someone wasn't satisfied with their meal, we made them another one. We refilled our soda glasses whenever we wanted. Whenever a new flavor of cheesecake came in from the distributor, we thought nothing of grabbing a slice to "taste test" but never considered we should pay for it. At the beginning of the shift, we grabbed a baked potato or a salad from our salad bar to scarf down before the rush. Everyone felt like they were part of it, and nobody meant any harm. Still, the lack of controls, standards, processes and oversight would be our undoing.

When we had to close our doors after over fifty years in business, it was devastating to me. I couldn't understand. What on earth could have destroyed such an amazing place and stolen my dream from me? As a kid, the restaurant felt like an unlimited resource. Customers kept coming, so why didn't the machine keep churning?

I would come to learn that if a restaurant does everything right: strong cost controls, efficient operations, solid labor management, surveillance and point-of-sale with loss prevention auditing, inventory control, and consistent sales, the percentage of gross sales that ends up as profit averages around five percent. That's not a lot of wiggle room for a mom-and-pop business.

Our business folded because of many years of unmanaged, poor controls and internal theft. Not awful food. Not a lousy location. Not incoming competitors. Essentially, it was the "Robbers." Trusted people to whom we gave the keys to the kingdom. Unknowing perpetrators who assumed ownership of the family restaurant because it was just "the way." All the years of free food and drinks were literally "on the house," and it was truly our undoing. The beast became so huge within our four walls that one day, it finally ripped us apart beyond repair.

When our restaurant closed, I worked at corporate restaurants for several years. But I grew exhausted with the hustle of the service industry life, and I decided it was time for a change. Back in those days, my dad owned a cash register company and had just added point-of-sale and surveillance solutions to his offering. Since I knew the restaurant and bar business, his world felt like the perfect fit for me. It was then that I began my career as a bar and restaurant consultant, working for my dad.

I spent the next 20 years working in the hospitality scene and advising on loss prevention, security and point-of-sale. The best part of the job was meeting so many amazing people and getting to be a part of their "dream." I got to try all the food. I was invited to all the grand openings. The restaurants we worked with all treated me like family. I gained forty pounds during that chapter of my life! I simply couldn't say "no" to the owners that proudly offered me dish after dish.

The worst part of the job was seeing people inevitably taken advantage of. Owners who trusted their friends and family ended up losing their money…and their dreams. Our company's technology tracked the cash, so we often had to deliver the bad news and uncomfortable truth that the most "trusted" had been untrustworthy. It was never pretty, telling people there was a "robber" in their midst.

During my tenure, I helped countless restaurants, bars and nightclubs catch theft within their operations. I can tell you from personal experience that nine times out of ten, the culprit was always the closest and most beloved employee, sometimes even ownership partners. Many times, the restaurant had lost tens of thousands of dollars before anyone detected the theft. In several of the cases that I investigated, the restaurant lost hundreds of thousands of dollars.

It didn't matter how many times I warned people. It seemed impossible for business owners to consider that someone they loved could steal and intentionally harm them.

During my consulting career, I worked predominantly with mom-and-pop operations. My hospitality upbringing, personal experience and passion to help the independent restaurant owner made me extremely successful in my job. Many times, the people that I worked with were first-time owners. Many were opening their restaurants after decades of working full-time jobs in corporate America. They would finally realize their dream using retirement accounts including 401(k) money and other life-long savings.

> *So many people dream of owning a restaurant.*
> *Few people realize what that dream entails.*

Seldom is a restaurateur prepared to become a loss prevention expert. I have never once seen the role of "robber catcher" included in the dream scenarios my clients have proudly shared with me as they have prepared to open their restaurants. Very few showed awareness of the looming threats that were facing them from within the four walls of their "dream" businesses.

I've seen restaurants dissolve their operations and close the doors altogether to get out of partnerships with thieving co-owners. I've seen restaurant owners prosecute their best friends, and run away from the industry forever because they are so disgusted with the experience they've had.

> *Dreams go down the drain.*
> *Money goes down the drain, too.*

Nobody wants to hear that the people they've hired or partnered with are stealing from them. I have often consulted with restaurant owners who were appalled at the mere suggestion that someone on their team would be dishonest. For them, the idea of having a thief on the payroll was an insult to their intelligence and ability to judge character.

Unfortunately, internal theft is one of the biggest threats facing owners in the hospitality industry today. It doesn't discriminate. If you are in the restaurant business, people will steal from you. "The robbers" are hiding in plain sight.

To this day, almost thirty years later, I grieve what was and what could have been with my family's restaurant. I tell my son about my days growing up there, the fun times I had and how I wish things had turned out differently. I wanted to create this book to pay tribute to that family business and to protect other families from traveling down the same path that ours did.

I have partnered with the most intelligent, experienced, thoughtful, business-savvy expert I could find to present this data to you in a digestible way that will immediately transform how you approach your business. My partner's proven track record in successful business transformation coupled with my experience in the hospitality world combine to form a system of security you can implement immediately. Together, we aim to reveal the mind-blowing threats facing you today while we provide you with solid solutions and a plan to safeguard your business.

Now, let me pass the mic to Jauna...

Jauna's Story

When Chloe approached me about writing this book, I immediately knew it was a topic worth exploring. What I didn't realize is the ENORMOUS amount of theft that restaurateurs face. Now that I know, I can't help but imagine an owner surrounded by employees, friends, and family, ready to stab them in the back, much like Julius Caesar. The research and stories that we found range from SMH to OMFG.

As Chloe's gut-wrenching story perfectly captures, theft can quickly take a restaurant and the owners into the red, causing hardship both in the short-term and, sometimes, for years after the business closes. So, I was surprised to see how few people and groups in the industry are talking about theft as an operational and financial threat. Not only are knives out for owners, there is a lack of information on how to protect yourself, which is why we have devoted our time and energy to fill that gap.

Coincidentally, my professional journey started in restaurants. Like a lot of young people in the US, I started out as a bus person, a hostess and a fast-food staffer. It was also my introduction to a career in business optimization. I didn't realize it at the time but the layout of Taco Bell's line and the very specific training on how to build that taco (lettuce with your right hand, cheese with your left at the same time) was not only keeping our order times down but also making my job on the line less stressful because the line design and process could keep up with orders.

Just as Taco Bell made it less stressful to do my part-time job, I've seen throughout my business career that the workplace has a much larger impact on people's lives than just the hours they spend at work. Better work and working conditions often lead to better physical and mental health for team members, which, by extension, leads to healthier families and even healthier communities.

I know it sounds a little idealistic, but I firmly believe that improving people's lives at work is a small way to make life better for everyone in the community.

With that mantra in mind, I've become a passionate advocate for improving processes and associated IT solutions for businesses. That sounds as exciting as watching paint dry for most people, and sometimes it is.

But here's the cool thing for you as a business owner or manager. When you optimize your business processes correctly, you also improve the customer experience. This can increase your restaurant's profitability.

So, when you work to make your team's day easier and better, you're also driving your own success. When you protect your business from theft, you protect your staff as well. Sometimes from their own poor decisions but mainly by ensuring that you can continue to give them hours and pay as a profitable business.

That's why my approach to business optimization always starts with people. Focus on what your customers want and what your team needs. Second, develop and keep improving processes to help your team deliver the food and service with ease, even on your busiest days. Third, find technology/systems that lock in those processes so the technology is constantly reinforcing the process and making your job easier with more transparent operations because of automation, reporting, alerts, etc.

We are glad that you have pulled up a seat and are ready to learn more about this enormous risk to your livelihood. Let's dig in.

HOW WE RESEARCHED

To give you the best information, we dove deep into existing studies, industry group reports, etc. We also conducted a nationwide (US) proprietary survey and dozens of interviews with current and former owner/operators, hospitality industry experts, loss prevention experts and hospitality vendors to bring you the "Word On the Street." We hunted down stories reported in the news for insight into how widespread and damaging theft can be for a restaurant or bar, and you will see these stories in the "Newsworthy" sections.

Along with that information, we collected solutions that range from simple checklists to implementing new management applications, so there are ideas for every size restaurant and every budget. You can also jump on our website, www.howistealfromyou.com, to find more resources, stay informed of trends in hospitality-industry theft and find vendors and service providers that can help you.

CAST OF CHARACTERS

To keep it easy to remember and implement solutions, we have identified different types of theft with criminal "villains." With a chapter devoted to each of these characters, you can choose to reference this book to eliminate a specific type of theft that you are experiencing or read the chapters in order for a systemic review of your current risk areas and ways to identify and eliminate theft that frequently occurs in restaurants.

All the information we are giving empowers restaurant owners and managers to protect their dreams. Use it as a weapon to defend yourself against the attacks that will inevitably come. Arm yourself so that you can survive when so many people are trying to take advantage of you. It isn't a case of "if." It is very much a case of "when."

Maybe you aren't there yet, but you dream of one day owning a bar or restaurant: this book is required reading for your future success. We have researched and curated the content in this book with a genuine passion for the hospitality industry. We believe that if we can save "just one" restaurant by educating hospitality owners and managers with the information in this book, then writing it was time well spent.

If you are holding this book, please understand that it's not a coincidence; you are meant to have it in your hands. There is a reason this knowledge has been given to you. Do not shrug it off and set it aside for "later". Please make it a priority to digest this information and use it to your benefit immediately.

We give this to you with love and best wishes for you and your families to have many generations of success, amazing memories, happy customers and uncompromised profits.

Now, buckle up for these unbelievable but true "Stories of the Robbers."

CHAPTER 2
A DAY IN THE LIFE - JACK AND JILL'S GASTROPUB

Many people picture a thief very specifically in their minds. A bandit. A bank robber. A shoplifter. A Wall Street embezzler. Some folks can only imagine a thief in these specific contexts... and they only associate theft with the stealing of cash or merchandise from a bank or retail shop. For that reason, we thought it might be helpful if we painted a picture for you of "A Day in the Life" at a typical restaurant. For some, this story will resonate, and for others, it will be an eye-opener.

For this tale, we will go inside a fictional restaurant - Jack and Jill's Gastropub. The scenarios presented show the scope of what a typical owner/operator faces in their day-to-day operations. What happens at Jack and Jill's will be validated by dozens of true stories, interviews and mind blowing, verifiable data that we will share later on with you in this book.

Bon appétit!

It's Wednesday morning at 7:59 AM, and at Jack and Jill's Gastropub, Don, the kitchen manager, arrives to unlock the back door of the restaurant. Several employees are already waiting to get inside and start their prep work for the opening lunch shift. Once Don opens the door, the crew rushes to the time clock. Maymie clocks herself in, also taking the liberty of clocking in her roommate, Susan. She knows Susan is running 15 minutes late and can't afford to miss the time. Brandy puts on a pot of coffee, and everyone gets to their workstations as the day begins!

Don wraps potatoes in foil, Maymie chops cabbage for the coleslaw, Brandy boils water for eggs, and Jake is forming burger patties. Susan gets to the restaurant over 25 minutes late, but nobody's mad because she brought donuts. She grabs herself a cup of coffee and starts baking the bread.

At 9 AM, the food truck arrives with the day's delivery. Don has been with Jack and Jill's for over ten years, and he has an outstanding relationship with the food vendors. He manages all the ordering for the back of the house and maintains the inventory counts. Don opens the back door for the delivery man, and they walk to the cooler to check in the order. As he is counting the meat with the vendor, Don realizes that there is an extra ten-pound beef tenderloin in the order. Although he verifies on the invoice that Jack and Jill's is getting charged for the beef even though he didn't order it, Don doesn't include it in his count and just places it on the shelf for later. Don's wife has a small catering business, and she can use the tenderloin for her gig on Friday night. Winning!!!

At 10:30 AM, Jake makes a small huevos rancheros casserole for the kitchen staff to scarf down before the restaurant opens, and Susan preps the expo line. The bread is fresh out of the oven and warm, so everyone has a hot slice of it with butter to accompany their huevos rancheros while they take a quick break to eat.

For the lunch shift, there will be six servers on the floor and one bartender. Most servers will arrive at 11:30 AM, but Juan and Kelly arrive at 10:30 to make the tea and coffee, roll the silverware, and prepare the front of the house for the guests.

Kelly goes to the walk-in to get out the ketchup, and she grabs some prosciutto from the bin for a quick snack while she's in there. There wasn't time for breakfast this morning, and she needs her protein. She also grabs a hard-boiled egg with the bottles of ketchup, and she's out the door. Juan checks the wait stations out front and fills a Styrofoam cup with a Red Bull from behind the bar because he knows he's gonna need the extra kick for today's shift. He makes one for Kelly too because teamwork makes the dream work, and that's how they roll.

As the restaurant opens at 11 AM, Sean, the assistant manager, arrives and unlocks the office to get the cash drawer out of the safe. He counts the cash, including his IOU slip for fifty bucks, the money he borrowed yesterday, and preps the bar drawer with $250.

The house-specialty brownies are being pulled from the oven, and they smell SO good. Sara, the hostess, is in the kitchen getting herself a soda for the shift, and while she is back there, she begs Jake for a brownie. He happily obliges and discreetly passes it to her across the line. Sara takes her drink and her treat up to the hostess stand to snack on while she waits for the first guests.

Darren, the bartender, arrives ten minutes late and skips the time clock. He'll write in his time when he clocks out. He goes to the office to collect the drawer from Sean and rushes to open the bar. Darren also needs a Red Bull to function today. He doesn't have time to do a proper count of the bottled beer, but he closed last night, so it's all good. The drawer is over by five dollars, but Darren just pockets it so he can quickly balance his drawer before the first customer comes in the door. He rushes to chop his limes and oranges and sets up the well. It looks like Juan iced the beer tubs for him already and turned on the margarita machine. Darren takes note and will hook Juan up later for his efforts. The crew at Jack and Jill's look out for each other because here, everyone is like family. Darren does a quick check of the surrounding scene and, yes, the bar is now OPEN!

Mike, Michelle, Faith and JJ arrive at 11:30 AM to complete the waitstaff roster for the lunch run today. They all go to Sara so she can show everyone their sections and then disperse with some grabbing themselves a drink for the shift. Michelle grabs a few rolls and butter from the kitchen for the gang to munch on while they wait for their tables to fill. The bread tastes extra amazing. Kelly and Juan already have a few tables, and with the gorgeous weather, it looks like it's going to be busy today.

The pub is hopping, and by noon, there's a full house! Everyone wants to sit in Kelly's section, but it is already full, and she's totally slammed. Of all the servers at Jack and Jill's, Kelly has been there the longest. All of her "call customers" love her because she takes such good care of them, like they're family. Kelly is such a rockstar that she can handle a five-table section with ease, and even if she gets in the weeds, she never lets 'em see her sweat.

Kelly seldom charges for tea or soda instead ringing it up as water on the POS system. After all, it barely costs Jack and Jill anything for tea and coke and the customers tip better when they notice they don't have to pay for their drinks. Kelly always offers her guests a fresh "to-go" cup for the road, and they love her for it. Today during lunch, Kelly turned her tables twice. Her headcount for the shift is 38 guests, and she clears a hundred bucks in tips! A little extra ranch and a little extra love go a long way and make Kelly a "fan favorite" at Jack and Jill's.

Juan has a different method of operating his section. Being the computer whiz that he is, Juan rings up four beverages for table twelve and prints a copy of the check. Then, he moves the drinks off of the table twelve check to another open table on the POS. When they are ready to pay, Juan presents table twelve with his preprinted guest check, which includes the four beverages, and they pay cash and tell him to keep the change. He closes the sale out for table twelve on the POS system, but remember, the beverages have already been safely moved to the other table's check because they ordered four drinks too. Because the guest check Juan closes out is missing the drinks that the customers have just paid for, he can make an extra fourteen bucks on top of his tip for the cash paying customers thanks to his brilliant method of moving the drinks off before settling their check. Juan is a genius. Granted, he can only pull this off three times today because everyone else paid with credit cards...but he makes an extra forty-two bucks ON TOP OF HIS TIPS during the lunch shift just by getting creative and doing the soda shuffle!

One server, Sean's buddy Mike, is not having a good day today. He just got dumped and has a hell of a hangover. Mike spends his entire shift visibly in the weeds, and his tips are clearly a reflection of his crummy performance. He knows for sure he is getting a bad Google review from one table full of women in the corner- they hate his guts. If all four do separate nasty reviews, it won't surprise him.

Mike complains to Sean that he has already been stiffed on his tips twice during the shift and Sean, being the cool guy that he is, reopens a closed check and comps a couple of apps citing the reason as "unhappy guest," which gives Mike an extra twenty bucks. Mike closes out his section and calls it a day, and Sean tells Darren to pour Mike a draft beer and not to worry about ringing it up. He pats Mike on the back, telling him to shake it off. Everyone has a bad shift once in a while and tomorrow is a new day. At Jack and Jill's, everyone takes care of each other.

The lunch rush is over by 2 PM, and except for Darren, Sara and Faith, the front of house lunch shift is over. Even though the restaurant was busy, Darren has only had a few regulars today, and he's pretty sure all hope is lost on clearing a hundred bucks for his shift. Suddenly, the 3 PM crew from the office next door comes in for one of their famous afternoon "meetings," which include drinks and apps paid on a corporate card. Darren knows these guys will make the shift worth it today, so he goes the extra mile for them.

At the bar, Darren makes their drinks in a dramatic fashion, ensuring the office crew sees his generous pours. Darren tells them they deserve it for their loyalty to Jack and Jill's. The fans go wild!

For two hours, Darren takes extra special care of the guests including a free basket of chips and salsa, some heavy pours and a little charm as they run up a two hundred dollar tab! As expected, one of the office crew whips out his corporate card to pay, and Darren closes out the check. They tip Darren forty bucks, but Darren knows he can turn the zero in the 40 into an eight on his copy of the receipt and at least get a little more. No one will ever notice.

It's 4 PM and Don is done for the day. He makes himself a burger to go and gets Darren to ring it up for him, applying the employee discount to the transaction. Darren, being one of the most trusted employees at Jack and Jill's, has the authority in the POS system to apply discounts to checks. When Don pays, Darren uses his own personal loyalty reward card and grabs a few reward points for the transaction. Don packages up his burger, puts it in a plastic bag and stops by the walk-in to grab the tenderloin on his way out the door. Beef in the bag, he pops his head in the office door and says bye to Sean as the bar manager, Kim, and some of the night crew arrive. It's almost time for a shift change in the front and back of the house.

The trash is overflowing, so Jake grabs the bin to take it to the dumpster. On his way to the door, Jake stops by the walk-in and grabs a six-pack of IPA from the cooler and adds it to the trash bin, under a little garbage. Jake gets to the dumpster and carefully places his six-pack behind the enclosure, where nobody can see it, and then empties the bin and heads back in to do his closing work.

It's 4:30 PM and Sean has officially taken in all the checkouts for the day from the servers. Kelly had such a busy section and quite a few cash-paying customers. Sean goes to a POS terminal and comps out an $80 cash transaction from Kelly's section citing a "bug in the food" as the reason for the comp. Sean reruns Kelly's cash out report so that he can then pull $80 cash from her cash out and replace his IOU slip from the safe bag. The extra thirty bucks is gravy. It was a long shift today, and he earned it.

Ten minutes later, Jake finishes for the day. Brandy is on her way out the door and refills her drink for the road before she clocks out and hits the bricks. Jake clocks out and on his way to his car he grabs the six-pack from his secret hiding spot behind the dumpster. Maymie and Susan take off their aprons and pony up to the bar to order their employee meal from Darren. He rings it up and applies the employee discount, and swipes his loyalty reward card again to build up some more rewards for himself while they sit at the bar and drink a margarita, waiting for their food. Of course, Darren is not gonna charge the girls for their drinks because it's frozen sugar, nobody's counting it, they are total sweethearts and their hard work makes the world go round at Jack and Jill's. Faith delivers the food to Maymie and Susan, and they sit and munch for an hour while drinking and chatting about the insane shift they just survived.

Sean stops by the bar to talk with Kim and make sure she is prepared for the evening shift. Jack and Jill are supposed to be coming in tonight for dinner and drinks with friends, and he wants to give her the heads up and make sure they get a great server and the best table. More night shift servers and hostesses are arriving through the back door along with the dishwasher and kitchen line crew. Maymie and Susan finish up their meals. They say their goodbyes and clock out at 5:30 PM on their way out the door.

It's the end of Darren's shift so he rings up a burger and applies the employee discount to his meal and then uses his loyalty reward card not only to get credit for the purchase but also to apply some of his reward points to his check. As part of the exceptional loyalty reward program at Jack and Jill's, with every hundred dollars you spend, you get a five-dollar credit on your loyalty card to apply to a later purchase. Darren always uses his own loyalty reward card when he's ringing up employee meals so he has a nice piggy bank full of rewards to apply to his own transactions whenever he needs them. By using the employee discount coupled with some rewards points, Darren can get his meal for free today, as usual. He hands over the bar to his manager, Kim, and another bartender, Jason, after counting down his drawer. Darren turns the drawer over to Kim with his checkout and then sits at the bar and eats while visiting with Sean about the lunch shift. Sean leaves at 6 PM, and Darren ends up leaving around 6:30 and clocks out on his way out the door.

It's 7 PM and the proud owners of Jack and Jill's Gastropub, Jack and Jill, arrive with Jill's brother Dick and his wife Jane for a delicious dinner. Jane is also the accountant who handles all the payroll and finances for Jack and Jill's Gastropub. Jack has always believed that it's best to keep the business in the family when you can.

Kim makes sure that Jack and Jill sit in Karen's section tonight. Karen is an all-star and will give the proud owners and their guests impeccable service. Tonight, Jane is proposing to Jack and Jill that they move to a new credit card processor. Jane has run the numbers and says that she can save Jack and Jill $200 a month or $2400 a year if they make the switch. Jack assures Jane that whatever she thinks is best for the business is good with him, and he tells her to sign the paperwork. Karen brings over a bottle of Jack's favorite wine to the table with four glasses and a heaping basket of fresh hot rolls. They pour the wine.

Manny is one of the closing servers on the shift tonight, and he is as much of a rockstar as Kelly was at lunch. At 7:30 PM,

Manny has a full section and is upselling like a boss. The key to Manny's success is turning his tables as much as possible and offering to take extra tables when other servers are ready to go home and get cut. He can always use the extra tip money because his wife is pregnant, and kids aren't cheap. Manny has to make money wherever he can. Thankfully, Manny purchased a little device from the internet that he keeps in his apron pocket. The device is Manny's second job and acts as his second income. Whenever Manny is closing out a table, he can quickly tap any credit card that his customer gives him to the device, and it stores the credit card information for later. They want separate checks? EVEN BETTER. On a busy night, Manny can get 20 different credit cards, sometimes more if he is a closer. At the end of the weekend, Manny will use the device to dump all the credit card information into a file, and then he will sell the card numbers to his buddy and make an extra grand.

It's 8:30 PM, and the table next to Jack and Jill is not happy. They ordered some of the most expensive items off the menu, and much to their disappointment, there were hairs in two of the dishes. They complain loudly to Karen, and Jack overhears the commotion. The customer threatens to leave a scathing online review if the meal is not comped immediately. Jack stands up from his seat at the table and goes to greet the guests and apologizes profusely for their experience. He instructs Karen to get Kim to comp the entire check and to bring the guests one of each dessert "on the house." After all, Jack knows everyone decides where they're going to eat based on online reviews, and he cannot afford to lose the business if this customer tells her story to the world.

While Jack is talking to the unhappy customers, his sister-in-law, Jane, is discreetly texting her friend who works at the credit card processing company that will take over the payments for Jack and Jill's Gastropub. She lets her friend know the deal is done, and she will send over the paperwork tomorrow, and she includes a $ emoji for added enthusiasm. The credit card company has promised Jane that she can personally have a percentage of the credit card processing residuals if she moves the account. Even with the $200 monthly savings that Jane can provide to Jack and Jill's by moving their processing, she will make an extra $500 a month for herself from the deal and that's not even for the busy season. Jane sits at the table and quietly fantasizes about a European vacation if she can just get a few more of her clients switched over to this new processor while Jack wraps up placating the upset customer. Karen brings the desserts out of the kitchen for the hairy table, and they clean their plates.

Closing time approaches, and except for a few folks around the bar, business is winding down quickly. Kim cuts all the front-of-house servers except for Manny. Karen's disgruntled table leaves too, high-fiving each other for their awesome score once they reach their car. The good old "hair in the food gets a bad review" scam goes a long way, and tonight it got them a free $150 meal!!!

Most of the employees have ordered a meal and are waiting at the bar to eat. The hostesses have been sent home, and the kitchen staff is praying that no new orders come in once they finish cooking the servers' meals so they can shut down the show. Bart, one of the line cooks, drops a basket of fries and some wings so that everyone has something to snack on at the end of the night. It was a great shift, and everyone deserves a treat!

After they polish off a second bottle of wine, Kim closes Jack and Jill's entire guest check, adding an owner comp, and Jack and Jill stumble out the front door with Dick and Jane. Karen can finally go home, hallelujah! Jack left Karen a $100 tip on the table, like he always does. Jack and Jill are the salt of the Earth and they ALWAYS take care of their people.

Jack and Jill's Gastropub is officially closed for the night!

It's 10 PM, and the kitchen is so spotless that you could eat off the floor. Tonight's crew went the extra mile to clean up the back of the house and do a lot of prep work for tomorrow's shift. The kitchen crew packs up whatever is left of the wings and fries that Bart made in some to-go boxes, grab their bags, clocks out and leaves out the back door.

By 10:30 PM, the wait staff that is still lingering around the bar having cocktails after their finished shifts are getting rowdy. Jason has already done his beer count, his drawer count, his cleanup and his cash out. Kim announces she wants to go home, and it's time to end the day! Everyone quickly slams the rest of their drinks, and they all scurry to the time clock to clock out while Kim double-checks that the front doors are locked and the lights are off in the front of the house. Employees trickle out the back while Manny makes sure the wait stations are pristine for tomorrow's openers. The staff completed all the other side work earlier, making tonight's closing a breeze.

Kim locks the office up while Manny and Jason clock out, then sets the alarm and they all walk out the back door together. A quick fist bump and everyone goes their separate ways.

Another dollar, another day.

And what an awesome "Day in the Life" it truly was at Jack and Jill's Gastropub!

Let's check out the tab for today, shall we?

Guest Check

Date	Table	Guests	Server	0123456

1	Susan early clock in (25min at $18 p/h)	$7.50
1	Don's 10LB tenderloin	$200
1	Jake's Huevos Rancheros	$15
1	Bread for the A.M. staff	$5
1	Kelly's prosciutto	$1
1	Kelly & Juan's Red Bull	$5
1	Sarah's brownie	$3
1	Darren's 10 minutes late ($12 p/h)	$2
1	Darren's Red Bull	$2.50
1	Darren's $5 drawer overage	$5
1	Mike, Michelle, Faith & JJ shift sodas	$12
1	FOH server bread rolls	$2
1	Kelly's uncharged 20 beverages	$60
1	Juan's stolen beverages	$42
1	Mike's comp by Sean	$20
1	Mike's free draft beer	$5
1	Darren's office crew over pour	$10
1	Darren's tip manipulation	$8
1	Darren's free basket of chips & salsa	$5
1	Darren's loyalty thieving	$10
1	Jake's 6 pack at retail	$24
1	Sean's $80 comp of Kelly's check	$80
1	Maymie & Susan EOD clock riding	$36
1	Maymie and Susan's free margaritas	$10
1	Darren's EOD clock riding	$12
1	Unhappy customers check comp	$150
1	Unhappy customer dessert comps	$20
1	Jane's credit card kick back (500 p/m)	$16.44
1	Bart's wings & fries for the kitchen	$30
1	Lurking servers riding the clock @ EOD	$30
	TOTAL	**$828.44**

Once Manny's credit card data breach is discovered, Jack and Jill will also have to pay to replace each compromised card at a cost of $3-$10.
- and will likely be fined thousands of dollars for the data breach.

Thank You - Please Come Again

CHAPTER 3
SETTING THE TABLE

Like Jack and Jill, if you own, manage or work in the hospitality industry, you are likely brushing up against thieves and scammers frequently. Sometimes, the thefts are petty amounts that are barely noticeable in your normal expenses, so you may think it's not worth your additional time or money to do some active prevention. No point in spending $20 to save the $5 in soda that your team may steal, right?

Unfortunately, restaurant theft is big business for crooks, a lot bigger than just a couple of employees sneaking soda and brownies!

Starting at the top, the Association of Certified Fraud Examiners (ACFE) looked at 35 cases of theft in the food service/hospitality industry for their 2024 annual report on fraud[1].

The median loss for these 35 cases was $100,000.

Yep, $100k and, as the median, that means half of the cases of theft were above $100k, so that's not even the worst case.

To pile on here, theft causes a third of business bankruptcies in the US.[2] That's right, a third and business losses from these bankruptcies add up to ~$50 billion a year.

If we look at just the restaurant industry, internal theft in US restaurants costs an estimated $3-6 billion (with a b, *billion*) a year.[3]

Let's break those numbers down so it's easier to do the mental math of how much this could cost you and your restaurant(s).

ACFE estimates that companies *typically* lose 5% of their revenue to theft and fraud each year- five freaking percent! When the average restaurant is squeaking by on less than 6% margins, it's easy to see how quickly theft can take your bottom line from the black to the red.

WORD ON THE STREET

We interviewed a Midwestern point-of-sale provider and loss prevention expert about her experiences with clients that suffered from internal theft. She told us about an Ohio slider burger shop in Wyandot that opened with a counter-service model and no servers:

> "When they opened, their team started giving products away either for free or heavily discounted so as to encourage repeat business but there was no guideline for the team to use. It cost the business so much money that the owner ended up having to turn off all of the discounts within two weeks of his opening. The owner ended up firing all the team and he and his daughter became the only two employees. He asked us for help because they couldn't really run the restaurant with just the two of them but he was too scared to hire anyone after his experience after opening."

She continued:

"We put in QR codes for them to take orders which eliminated theft, comps and discounts by the cashier(s). However, it was too late to save the business. The existing customers of the new business now had an expectation for free and discounted food and drinks and stopped coming back. Within six months, he just couldn't stay open. It was a shame because he was such a nice guy, and the concept itself was really good. But he just got off to a bad start and, between not being able to trust hired team members and brand expectation damage, he had to close."

WHO TO TRUST...AND WHO TO WATCH

In our fictional story of Jack and Jill's Gastropub, it's easy to tell who's on the take and who's not, but we all know that real life is a lot more complicated. According to the California Restaurant Association, **75%** of all employees have stolen from their employer at least once.[5]

Let's put it another way: as you walk through your restaurant, 3 out of 4 of the people you say "hello" to are stealing from you or have stolen from you in the past.

In our research, we heard some business owners talk about the **"20/60/20 rule."** This industry anecdote suggests that approximately 20% of your team will always steal, ~60% might steal if given a chance, ~20% will never steal.

It would be comforting if the data confirmed that it's only new employees or serial offenders that we should watch the most. However, as one of our interviewees said, *"the more trusted the individual, the more they stole,"* and our survey results confirmed this with ~83% of the reported thefts being committed by someone the owner trusted. The ACFE also reports that the median cost of the theft/fraud goes up based on the tenure of the employee with incidents involving employees with over 10 years at the company likely to cost 5X the theft and fraud of a new employee (*$250k versus $50k median per incident*).[6]

That may seem like a head scratcher but it makes sense based on the access that your longer-tenured and, presumably, more trusted employees have.

Who are you trusting with the keys to the restaurant? To override controls in your POS system? Order inventory and manage your liquor vendor relationships? Run cash deposits to the bank? Who knows what controls are in place so they can also figure out how to get around them?

If you're now thinking: "Well, that sucks. I like all the people at my restaurant."

We hear you.

Life would be much easier if good rapport and tenure were enough to vouch for someone's trustworthiness. But since that is not the case, every restaurateur should understand that the foundation for maintaining trust is having robust processes and systems that remove opportunities for theft and the punch-in-the-gut feeling of betrayal.

EVERY RESTAURANT IS AN OPPORTUNITY

Now, you may think that this doesn't really apply to you because *your restaurant is different*, even unique, so you don't have the same risk as other restaurants. You might believe this is a franchise problem linked to higher employee turnover, so it doesn't apply to you because your team has been with you for a long time. Or, flipping the perspective, it's a small restaurant problem because, as part of a larger chain, you have better point-of-sale and surveillance solutions to prevent theft.

Unfortunately, we have to burst this optimism bubble as well. All, and we do mean ALL restaurants, are vulnerable to theft. Let's do a quick rundown of some major restaurant types and why they can be an easy target for theft:

Franchises-

- High cash volume
- The fast pace can reduce or complicate oversight
- Large percentage of young and/or inexperienced team members
- Management focused on speed (*watch that drive-in timer!*) not security

Independent Sit-Downs-

- Owners are often absent or overworked during operating hours
- Don't have corporate help with systems and procedures
- "Family atmosphere" that typically means fewer controls
- Cash tips and handwritten orders still allowed

Bars and Nightclubs-

- High Cash Volume
- Over-pouring is common and often unchecked
- Bartenders often handle both drink preparation and the register

Delivery or Takeout Heavy-

- High-volume of orders
- Orders can be marked incomplete while the team or other customers take the food
- Fake delivery failures and other chargebacks

We could go on, but you get the picture. The trick to protecting yourself is understanding where your vulnerabilities are and putting a strategy in place that is realistic and effective. We will help you out with that…just keep reading.

PARTY OF TWO...OR THREE...OR?

Theft is often a "team sport" within an independent restaurant, chain or local city. Nothing like having them gang up on you, right?

Teamwork in scams leads to bigger losses. When two or more team members work together, they steal more money. The median loss is around $329,000. This is compared to a median of $75,000 for solo thieves.[7] Theft rings are behind the most expensive and longest heists, especially in chains and franchises.

That increase in loss isn't just because more than one person means more theft has to occur so everyone can get a slice of the ill-gotten gains. It's also because it takes longer to detect the theft. Multiple people can override systems more easily (especially if one is a manager or supervisor) and cover for each other if anyone asks questions.

We will cover these types of theft in later chapters, but here's a short list of heists that need a partner or a team:

- Buddy punching - one person clocks in or out for another
- Cash register skimming - server under-rings and manager ignores it
- Free food for tips- the kitchen team prepares the order even if it wasn't rung in, and they split the fat tip they receive for giving the customer "free" food.

In our research, we came across many stories of team members, customers and even owners and partners working together to steal. We even heard a story of the owner's spouse working a theft scheme with a bartender who was also their affair partner! Yikes! It doesn't happen often, but it happens, which means you have to watch your partners and family members as well as your team.

Now, some of these employee theft rings or partnerships may form outside of the time the people worked at your restaurant and, sometimes, the rings will deliberately target businesses in a specific area to run their scams. Keep in mind, you are also at risk of a partnership or ring growing at your own restaurant, especially if you are not actively and consistently detecting and addressing theft.

A study conducted by Olin researchers at Washington University looked at seven years of data from 1,049 locations of 34 different casual dining restaurant chains in 46 states. The database included over 5.7 million transactions involving over 83,000 servers. *Pretty solid study...*

They found that theft is contagious or, in the study's language, exposure to a high-theft employee increased the chances that other employees would steal. The study also found that your newest employees (between 5-7 months of tenure) are the most susceptible to getting infected.[8]

Remember when we mentioned it takes longer for a multi-person theft to be discovered? This study showed that the teams work together to keep the theft under the radar by some members stealing less in a day if they noticed that another person in their ring was taking more than usual.[9] Way to look out for each other! So, if you have one rotten apple in your team bushel, you will not only lose money from that person, but it can infect the entire basket and the cost of that theft can quickly multiply.

Frequent monitoring is necessary to enable rapid response, so you must put in specific technology and processes to detect theft as quickly as possible! Prevention can also avoid the costs of firing multiple and possibly *prosecuting* multiple team members, not to mention the cost of hiring and training their replacements.

NEWSWORTHY

In Georgia, WALB 10 TV News reported that a local sheriff's office was asked to investigate four employees of a local iHOP restaurant after the restaurant's corporate headquarters found evidence of theft. Once the sheriff's office confirmed the estimated $21,000 theft outlined in the provided reports, the four suspects were arrested and are now awaiting criminal charges.[10]

PROTECTING YOUR BUSINESS WHILE KEEPING IT POSITIVE

While there are some serial thieves out there who are constantly looking for their next job and mark, we believe that most thieves are good people who are making poor decisions. *Spoiler alert: most thieves like to think they are good people too. We will explore the mindset of thieves throughout the book.*

Andy Grove, the late CEO of Intel Corp., famously wrote a book called "Only the Paranoid Survive." This advice can serve restaurateurs and managers because the reality of theft in restaurants and bars is grim shit. That being said, we aren't suggesting that you side-eye everyone, compulsively count registers and cross-examine the team every shift.

We actually do NOT recommend that approach. In fact, there is research that shows it might actually drive MORE theft as there is a correlation between working conditions and employee theft. In plain language, if the work culture sucks, employees are more likely to steal.[11]

Here's the kicker though. Since the people you trust are also more likely to steal from you, a long-term, positive relationship and/or ongoing friendship outside of work or family relationships can actually lead to *entitlement* that drives theft. We are talking about the cousin that you gave a job to as a favor who thinks of the restaurant as *"ours"* since it is *"family-owned."* In this cousin's mind, there's no problem taking $100 from the till as *"family helps family."* Never mind that they didn't invest a dollar in the business, have no ownership, liability or responsibility and won't be the one losing their house if the restaurant goes under.

THE GOOD NEWS

The trick is to set up your handbook, procedures and technology to be paranoid for you. As a long-time restaurateur told us during his interview:

> "...what a lot of restaurateurs fail to do is set standards. So, there's three ways a restaurant is most likely going to fail. And one of those three ways is the lack of systems and processes."

This is especially true in detecting and addressing theft. Make the investment in time and money to put the right processes in place, follow them consistently and insist that your team, vendors and partners also follow them.

With controls and monitoring working for you, you can still invite your managers over for the Sunday game, shake hands, chitchat with your team, and keep a positive environment because you know if somebody steals, you have the processes to catch them and quickly deal with it.

We are here to help!

At the end of each chapter in this book, we will give you tips on how to detect and prevent theft. We also encourage you to visit the "How I Steal From You" webpage (www.howisteal fromyou.com) for more resources and links, because everyone can appreciate an "easy button" to get started!

Now, for the tough part. Once you put systems and processes in place...you, your fellow owners and your managers have to follow and enforce them! Follow them consistently, diligently and quickly address any issues no matter how hard it is.

This includes putting a process in place to review your systems and processes periodically. Always work to improve! If you find theft in the restaurant that your current processes didn't detect *or* when you hear about the latest bartender scam at a local restaurant association meeting, it's time to make adjustments!

Look, we know investigating and dealing with a team member who is stealing is like walking through the third ring of hell. We know because we found many reports of restaurateurs and managers looking the other way or rationalizing and not dealing with the problem. It's human nature to want to avoid tough conversations or deal with having to replace and train new team members. But, as the research shows, it is essential that theft be detected as early as possible and then addressed as soon as possible.

*It's that simple...*and it's that hard.

HOW TO DETECT: BIG PICTURE

Here's the basic list of what you need. If you don't have this stuff, you're dead in the water. If you already have all of this in place, cheers! You're well on your way!

- Put together a loss prevention plan. This can be as formal as a standard operating procedure (SOP) or as simple as a checklist but get a plan in writing.
- If you have a Point-Of-Sale (POS), work with your POS vendor to take advantage of all the theft prevention features available to you, including understanding all standard or custom reports that are available.
    - By the way, it's good to make this a standard quarterly discussion with your vendor as they are a resource for staying on top of new scams and prevention features.
- Institute or update an employee handbook to address the rules and consequences of theft.
- Write daily, weekly and/or monthly procedures or checklists to ensure all of your theft prevention audits, video surveillance, reports, etc. are clearly defined.
- Train your team.
    - One note of caution here- While it might seem prudent to train everyone on everything, knowing all the procedures makes it easier for them to know how to get around detection if they decide to steal. You should train on a "need-to-know" basis and keep some tasks/reports, etc., for yourself as the owner/operator.
- Install surveillance cameras EVERYWHERE! It doesn't have to be a big fancy system, although go for it if you have the budget! Cameras are cheap to set up. Just to give you an idea, we recommend that a small restaurant should have a minimum of 36 cameras to ensure you have full coverage of the restaurant and areas where theft can occur. This includes your parking lot!

HOW TO PREVENT: DAILY DILIGENCE

- Build your theft prevention processes into your daily, weekly and monthly routine as an owner. Since you can't delegate this task entirely, integrate it into your restaurant routine, daily close, payment reconciliation, and other tasks for consistent completion.

Now that we have set the table for you, grab your popcorn (and your barf bag) and get ready to take a deep dive into this true crime saga!

CHAPTER 4
CROOKED CLOCKERS

Remember "A Day In The Life" at Jack and Jill's when Susan and Maymie sat at the bar, drinking margaritas on the clock? Or earlier in the day, when Maymie clocked her roommate, Susan, in on time even though Susan was almost half an hour late for work? When Darren skipped the time clock to avoid getting caught for showing up late? Remember when Darren ate his meal and socialized at the bar for an hour before clocking out and leaving for the day? Or at the end of the day when the night crew drank cocktails on the clock and then punched out on their way out the back door?

These employees are Crooked Clockers! In a single day, they cost the restaurant almost a hundred dollars. Do the math for yourself and you will see that if this is the typical behavior for these employees, they are likely bleeding Jack and Jill for thousands of dollars a year with their Crooked Clocking.

WHAT IF THERE ARE CROOKED CLOCKERS PUNCHING YOUR CLOCK?

Even one employee stealing ten minutes of time from you for every shift they work adds up to big bucks at the end of the month and we know it isn't a problem of just "one." **Statistics suggest that Crooked Clocking is one of the most potent and widespread forms of theft in the industry.** *More on that in a minute.*

You know what you pay your people, so you do the math! The numbers add up fast, and in this business, every single penny counts.

Time is money, literally!

THE UNCOMFORTABLE TRUTH

The American Payroll Association suggested in 2021 that companies can lose as much as **7% of their gross annual profit** through time theft.[1] The same report suggested that this statistic holds true for **75% of businesses in the United States.**[2]

Imagine the damage that time fraud could do to *your business!!!*

As we mentioned earlier, a restaurant will average only profit 5-6% at best *if they do everything right.*[3] So, a mom-and-pop restaurant could be utterly ruined if they have Crooked Clockers on their team.

The good news is that with proper controls in place, bar and restaurant owners can easily prevent Crooked Clocker theft.

HOW I STEAL FROM YOU 39

NEWSWORTHY

Time card fraud is one of the most difficult forms of theft for a restaurateur to prosecute criminally. Most hospitality theft prosecutions that make the news are about cash, tips, or embezzlement; where actual "time theft" cases more often get handled internally or via civil/administrative wage claims, not criminal court. This doesn't mean it isn't happening. It simply means there is little to no legal recourse for you, the victim. The best fighting chance you have to defeat the Crooked Clocker is to arm yourself with knowledge and be proactive with prevention.

We found some absolutely shocking Crooked Clocking News in the state of Pennsylvania. These mind-blowing stories will truly open your eyes to the magnitude of sinister behavior that occurs around the clock!!!

Pennsylvania

> Multiple news outlets reported in July 2019 that a general manager at an IHOP in Hempfield Township literally created a fake employee in the system and added shifts remotely to their time card. The same general manager was also adding shifts for a terminated worker. They determined that the loss was between $10-13,000!!![4]

Pennsylvania Again!

> Business Insider reported in July 2023 that Wendy's in Lancaster County had the same awful issue as the IHOP. The general manager was manually clocking a fake employee in and out for 128 fake shifts. The net loss was between $16- 20,000. The manager created a ghost employee that she regularly clocked in and out when she was at the restaurant. The Crooked Clocker

ran this scheme for almost a year before someone caught it in a formal audit.[5]

Poor Pennsylvania...

In Westmoreland County, CBS News reported in July 2025 that another IHOP location was suffering at the hands of a completely different Crooked Clocking manager. This manager faked an identity, entered 18 shifts, and endorsed paychecks by mobile deposit. They also added shifts for an ex-employee. The interesting thing is that during the investigation, police discovered the manager had been prosecuted at a former job for doing the same thing. If someone had actually checked the background and references of this person before they hired them, they could've avoided the entire mess.[6]

WORD ON THE STREET

We reached out to some hospitality owners and managers to get their feedback on Crooked Clockers. Check out what they had to say for ideas to help defend your business against this kind of criminal!

Michigan

We interviewed one bar owner from Detroit, who struggled with managing her labor costs. The owner discovered her employees were swapping shifts to get overtime pay. This savvy operator nixed the Crooked Clocking by implementing a scheduling program that prevented the scam from continuing in her business.

"Once I put employee scheduling software in place that integrated with my point-of-sale, I was able to control the bad behavior quickly. I made all of my employees sign a document stating that they would not swap shifts without management approval, and that there was a strict no overtime policy for our bar, moving forward."

It is common for servers to switch shifts without discussing their scheduling changes with management. It is up to you to set policies and procedures for shift swapping and using technology to manage the schedule will enforce the rules that you set. We understand that staffing can be a struggle in this industry and that working with the crazy schedules that employees have is cumbersome. This is why technology is the best solution to manage your labor costs and schedules, keeping Crooked Clockers from bleeding your business dry.

Texas

We spoke with a successful franchise owner from Dallas, who shared with us that they had major issues with buddy punching, specifically in the kitchen environment where their highest wage earners operated:

"We found that a lot of our kitchen staff members had relationships outside of the business, and as a result, they were accustomed to covering for each other to make sure they got as many hours as possible on their paychecks. We had to implement a biometric time clock to prevent our employees from clocking each other in. Investing in this technology paid for itself overnight."

If we shared with you every instance that we heard from business owners about buddy punching, this book would become so repetitive that you would put it down and walk away. When we tell you that this is an enormous problem in the hospitality industry, we are not exaggerating.

THE PERPETRATOR'S PERSPECTIVE

In the survey that we conducted on theft in the hospitality industry, one person shared a sentiment that is likely common amongst hospitality workers:

> "I was always late to work, but I would just skip the time clock because I could just tell my manager I forgot to clock in. This prevented me from getting in trouble for being late, and I never really thought about the fact that I was stealing money from the business by faking the time that I started working. I was just trying to not get in trouble for always running late for my shift."
> Steven, Denton TX

HOW TO PROTECT YOURSELF- YOUR DEFENSE CHECKLIST

Check out this "must have" list of solutions that you can use to guard yourself against labor fraud. You may already have some or all of these solutions in place. The question is: are you using the solutions to their full potential and auditing the data that is provided? And if you have none of these solutions.... It's time to make each one a reality in your operation! The longer you wait, the more you will lose.

- **Biometric time clocks-** Using fingerprint technology to clock in and out is a surefire way to prevent buddy punching. You can integrate this technology into some

point-of-sale and scheduling solutions, or it can stand alone in your operation.
- **Surveillance** is key to being able to reconcile what your employees tell you with the truth. If you can see when an employee walks in the door and when they actually finish working, you can pinpoint if there is dishonesty around when they punch the clock.
- **Scheduling software** empowers you to place controls around clocking in and clocking out, forcing manager approval for punches that occur outside of the thresholds you set for a specific employee's schedule. These can work with your point-of-sale or be standalone solutions.
- **Audit** your employee rosters on a consistent schedule. Make sure that the people you are paying to work are REAL human beings!
- **Policies and procedures** that are clearly communicated to your employees around their schedules will be key to your success.
  - **Shift swaps -** Managers should approve shift swaps to prevent unexpected overtime.
  - **Employee meals** should only be enjoyed once an employee can show they have clocked out.
  - **Strong rules** about clocking in early or clocking out late should be communicated in your handbook.
  - **Using scheduling software** to require management approval when employees navigate outside of the thresholds you have set will deter misbehavior.

SIGNS OF A CROOKED CLOCKER

In every interview that we conducted with industry experts, hospitality owners, and even the thieves themselves, there were always warning signs involved in their stories. If you pull off your rose-colored glasses, it may be easier to identify the perpetrators within your own four walls. Here are some common characteristics of Crooked Clockers. Watch for these red flags with your own team members. Ask yourself if you recognize these characteristics in anyone who works for you and use the information we are highlighting to identify potential areas of vulnerability:

$ **Crooked Clockers** may have a friend, roommate, romantic partner, or family member who is also working for the operation.

$ **Crooked Clockers** may frequently forget to clock in and out, requiring them to manually adjust their times with management.

$ **Crooked Clockers** may be people who arrive chronically late.

$ **Crooked Clockers** may be someone who constantly asks to get extra hours or to work overtime.

$ **Crooked Clockers** may stretch their work to get extra pay.

$ **Crooked Clockers** may have a payroll report that does not match their scheduled hours.

$ **Crooked Clockers** may take extended breaks, chat on the phone or linger after their shift is complete.

$ **Crooked Clockers** may *intentionally swap shifts* with colleagues to break into overtime.

$ **Crooked Clockers** often have an accomplice helping them manipulate timekeeping, and that accomplice may be unknowingly or consciously aiding the Crooked Clocker in their thievery.

FOOD FOR THOUGHT

A catering owner that we interviewed in Dallas, TX, shared with us her successful method for preventing buddy punching and overtime abuse in her kitchen where her labor costs were the highest:

"My entire baking team were salaried employees. This allowed me to offer schedule flexibility as an employee perk when we weren't busy and also allowed me to require my team to go the extra mile when we had a large order to put out. It protected me from people clocking each other in and riding the clock for overtime, and it also made my employees feel appreciated and that they were being paid what they were worth all the time. Putting this policy in place also guaranteed fixed labor costs when I was managing my business expenses."

THE FINAL DISH ON "CROOKED CLOCKERS"

Crooked Clocking is an obvious threat facing hospitality owners. Labor theft in restaurants and bars is a "tale as old as time" and a damning one. As the stories in this chapter show, some of these crooks are diabolically creative. Ghost employees?!?! *Who would have thought!!!*

It is very simple to protect yourself. Remember, your investment in the required technology will be minimal compared to the potential financial devastation if you do nothing.

REWARD

THE INVENTORY INFILTRATORS

CRIMINAL GANG AFFECTING INVENTORY COUNTS & THE BOTTOM LINE

THE BASIC BANDIT

USES THE POS TO MANIPULATE GUEST CHECKS

THE SWEETHEART

GIVES AWAY FOOD & BEVERAGES FOR A DISCOUNT OR FOR FREE

THE PRODUCT PINCHER

- STEALS PRODUCT AND SMUGGLES IT OUT OF THE BUILDING
- NOTORIOUS FOR HIDING THINGS IN OR AROUND THE DUMPSTER

THE MID SHIFT MUNCHER

CONSUMES FOOD & BEVERAGES ON THE CLOCK, WITHOUT RINGING THEM UP OR PAYING FOR THEM

CHAPTER 5
INVENTORY INFILTRATORS

While most of our "villains" standalone, we make an exception in this chapter and introduce a group of thieves together in one powerful kick to the proverbial balls. It's time to showcase one of the most nefarious criminal gangs in the hospitality industry today: **"The Inventory Infiltrators."**

This colorful cast of characters share the common bond of product thievery. These villains operate differently, and each one benefits differently from their theft, so their motives vary. However, they all negatively impact your inventory counts and your bottom line.

First, we will introduce **"The Sweetheart."** This Inventory Infiltrator gives away products or discounts to friends and family, often for no personal gain other than the enjoyment of their popularity and assumed ownership privileges. The Sweetheart sometimes does not even realize that what they are doing is theft. They may ring items up and discount them, or they may not ring the products up at all. Sometimes they will also give products away to complete strangers in order to get better tips.

The Sweetheart may even give away your chargeable goodies to other employees in order to boost their social cred with the team.

Next up is **"The Mid Shift Muncher."** This Inventory Infiltrator consumes products throughout the shift without ringing them up or getting a comp for the munchables. They don't pay for their snacks. Often, the Mid-Shift Muncher does not even realize that what they are doing is theft or causing any measurable harm. They have witnessed their colleagues having a bite here and there, and consider their consumption a benefit or "perk of the job."

We also have **"The Product Pincher."** *This thief knows exactly what they are doing, and they know it is wrong.* They remove valuable products from the business either to sell, give away, or consume off premise. Their theft typically affects a larger quantity of product. They smuggle goods out of the business in backpacks or garbage bins, and either sneak it to their cars or even hand it off to outside friends that drive by and pick it up.

Finally, we have **"The Basic Bandit."** This crook charges for products and gives them to the customer but keeps the cash for themselves. They know it's theft, and they act deliberately. Basic Bandits are committing double theft because not only are they giving your product away but they're also pocketing money. A Basic Bandit uses the point-of-sale system as a conduit for their crimes. They manipulate sales, comp checks after collecting cash, and move items from check to check. The Basic Bandit can be extremely damaging when they have stolen a manager's access code for the POS system. This access allows them to comp and void items or entire sales whenever they please.

Remember at Jack and Jill's when Juan and Kelly arrived for their shift and grabbed a Red Bull to energize themselves? Remember when Sarah got the brownie from Jake and when everyone was snacking on those delicious, warm rolls throughout the shift? Those folks were your typical Mid-Shift Munchers.

Remember when Darren gave the margaritas away to Maymie and Susan or when Kelly gave all the beverages away during her shift to get better tips? Those were your Sweethearts. Jake was a Sweetheart too when he gave the brownie to our Mid-Shift Muncher, Sara.

How about when Don took the tenderloin home for his wife's catering gig and when Jake snaked the six-pack of beer by the dumpster? That's right! Product Pinchers!!!

And don't forget when Juan moved his chargeable beverages from check to check, collecting payment for them from the customers, but not truly ringing them up for each individual table. Juan was a Basic Bandit.

Because inventory counting wasn't happening regularly at Jack and Jill's and because the managers are Snakes (a villain that we will cover soon), the Inventory Infiltrators can operate freely at the Gastropub. In one day, they took Jack and Jill for hundreds of dollars. It is actually a wonder that Jack and Jill's Gastropub is still open and probably just a matter of time before the whole thing comes crumbling down. The Inventory Infiltrators are playing a huge role in the inevitable demise of the business.

WHAT IF THE INVENTORY INFILTRATORS HAVE INFESTED YOUR INVESTMENT?

We're gonna break it to you gently...Inventory Infiltrators work for you today. The damage they are doing to your operation is likely significant.

Now that we have laid out all the ways that Inventory Infiltrators operate, the problem may seem overwhelming, especially when you reflect on scenarios that you have witnessed inside your own business. It may seem impossible to imagine being able to control or deter this kind of theft successfully. When we look at the entire picture, it might even make you question why you got into this business. **Don't despair.** This chapter is going to arm you with the information you need to have the upper hand against the Inventory Infiltrators and put a stop to their schemes quickly.

> "There is only one way to eat the elephant: one bite at a time."
> *Desmond Tutu, Bishop & Theologian*

THE UNCOMFORTABLE TRUTH

Loomis published a report in October 2025 that stated that employee theft accounts for 75% of product shortages in the hospitality industry.[1] It is absolutely impossible to measure how all of this theft is occurring–whether people are eating food from the line or in the walk-in, or just giving away products to be nice. Maybe the crooks are doing comps and voids and keeping the cash…maybe they are stealing the goods and taking them home. No matter what method the thieves are using, we know from the newsworthy cases we gathered in our research, as well as the anonymous reports from our survey, that the Inventory Infiltrators are likely the most dangerous entity inside of your business.

We also know this kind of theft is NOT a "one and done." It's recurring, and it spreads like a virus through the staff.[2]

Often, these behaviors go unseen or unchecked, with little to no accountability amongst the team. Often, the Snakes are major contributors to Inventory Infiltration. "Follow the Leader…."

> "If they do it often; it isn't a mistake- it's just their behavior."
> *Dr Steve Maraboli*

NEWSWORTHY

We put a lot of important stories in this chapter to make it clear: **DO NOT tolerate Inventory Infiltrators**. It is not a case of "maybe this is happening" at your establishment. The Inventory Infiltrators are operating their own enterprises inside of yours. See for yourself what others have found:

Las Vegas

> In February 2018, multiple news outlets published a story about product theft committed by a Product Pincher. A chef at the Bellagio smuggled $1875 worth of lobster tails out of the establishment. When you think about all the cameras and security inside a casino like The Bellagio, it's a wonder that the employee thought he could get away with his crustaceous heist. The chef was arrested and prosecuted for the crime. Even with the world's greatest surveillance solutions in place, thieves are still gonna thieve.[3]

Ireland

> In February 2025, the Belfast Telegram reported on an award-winning chef who stole over a thousand US dollars worth of alcohol and meat from a local restaurant named The Harbour House Inn. This Product Pincher was simply let go and slapped with a hefty fine.

> We suspect that many people worldwide get caught but are not prosecuted for this type of theft. That means that the restaurateur is never actually made whole. They never realize the full extent of the damage caused by the thieves that they catch and simply terminate.[4]

Florida

Fox 35 Orlando reported a mind-blowing case of internal theft in 2016. A server stole $32,751 from Red Bowl Asian Bistro. The Basic Bandit allegedly zeroed out food items and comped meals on cash checks. Not only was the food stolen and given away, but the cash was taken too. The server was charged with grand theft. He started stealing one month after his hire date, and the crimes went on for almost a year when the manager finally realized the Basic Bandit's sales were much lower than other employees' sales. The thief also admitted to offering bogus specials and discounts to guests hoping to pocket larger tips. What a Sweetheart![5]

It is not unusual for an Inventory Infiltrator to commit all the types of inventory theft at different times during their tenure. They give things away because they can. They munch on the line. They steal large quantities of products to take home or sell, and if the opportunity is there, they will manipulate the point-of-sale and steal cash while giving away products.

New York

In 2008, the New York Post reported on a Product Pincher who got busted at the famous restaurant, Junior's. This thief STUFFED 15 FROZEN LOBSTER TAILS DOWN HIS PANTS and into bandages tied around his legs![6]

The Product Pincher was a prep cook for the famous eatery, and a fellow kitchen crew member busted him. The employee saw the theft taking place and immediately called 911.

Wow. Just, WOW!

One has to wonder how many times this specific Product Pincher used his pants to smuggle goods out of the building. Because an *HONEST* employee (*one out of four, according to the statistics, don't forget*) spotted and reported the theft, the restaurant was no longer a victim to this pants artist and his Product Pinching schemes. Law enforcement charged the thief with petit larceny and criminal possession of stolen property.

If it hadn't been for one loyal employee paying attention at the right time, that guy in New York would have gone home with a heck of a lot of lobster tails down his pants. Which then makes us ask so many more questions.... Like, how did he smell? How did he sit down? How did he walk? How good does lobster actually taste after being bandaged up against a dude's sweaty, hairy legs... or did he shave first?

I guess we will never know...

London

> In September 2006, it was reported that one brave chef had the balls to steal from Gordon Ramsay! The chef, who worked at the Savoy Grill, attempted to smuggle out several hundred pounds worth of cookware from the Michelin-starred establishment. A copper saucepan, handmade crockery and expensive cutlery were all found during a random backpack check performed by restaurant security. The investigators believed that the Product Pincher had concealed the items during his break and planned to carry them out at the end of his shift. He was arrested but, even though he was not prosecuted, he is still forever branded with the reputation of trying to steal from one of the most famous and beloved restaurateurs in the world.[7]

It is important to remember that product theft is not just about food and alcohol. Employees will steal toilet paper, salt and pepper shakers, and restaurant equipment. We saw several instances online where former employees admitted to stealing proprietary recipes from their employers. A person who steals is going to take things whenever the opportunity presents itself.

New York

> The Twin Trees Too operation was hit hard in 2015, according to ABC News. A father and son team, who were cooks at the restaurant, ordered FORTY-ONE THOUSAND DOLLARS of chicken wings from the restaurant's wholesale provider and charged it on the restaurant's account!!! The dynamic duo picked up the wings from the wholesaler and resold them! The authorities charged both employees with grand larceny and falsifying business records.[8]

Unbelievable…. And the worst part? The father had **ALREADY** been arrested at a prior job for stealing. Stealing what, you may wonder? **Chicken wings!** A simple background check would have saved The Twin Trees Too the headache and extra work with all this "fowl play." Oh… and of course, it would have saved them forty-one grand.

In the research we did on this case, we could not establish if this scheme involved cooperation from the vendor, but it poses the question: did the vendor wonder what the heck was going on with these wings being ordered? Did they play a part in communicating with the restaurant owner and uncovering the chicken wing crime ring?

Florida

> Authorities busted a trusted employee at Home Plate on the Trail, a local Dunedin restaurant, for stealing $57,000, as

reported by WFLA in Florida. In typical fashion, the employee was canceling items on orders and pocketing the money. The scheme went on for years before the woman was caught. It took a forensic accountant and the suspicion of the restaurant owner to uncover the crimes.

Even though the restaurant carried out a three-day sting operation to catch the Basic Bandit in the act, when they busted her, she claimed ignorance and requested an attorney. Police found drugs in the employee's car when they finally arrested her, and they charged her with a scheme to defraud 50k or more, grand theft, possession of a controlled substance, and driving without a valid license.[9]

These "Newsworthy" stories prove several things: thieves are creative; they are bold; and in Inventory Infiltration, they go big or go home. These cases also show that employee awareness is important for discovering and stopping the Inventory Infiltrators. Vendor communication is vital. Random security bag checks are necessary, and surveillance doesn't matter if you don't audit or view it regularly.

WORD ON THE STREET

We interviewed several successful hospitality owners and managers about their own experiences with Inventory Infiltrators. They shared some helpful tactics for defense and we heard some very interesting stories along the way. Check them out!

Georgia

First, we interviewed a longtime entrepreneur who owned a well-known US breakfast franchise for many years. When we asked if he had any experience with Inventory Infiltrators, he shared this story:

> "It was funny. Our franchise had all the usual stuff when it comes to internal theft, but really, it was basic stuff that was affecting our bottom line. Bags of coffee. So many servers would grab bags of coffee to take home, just insane amounts of coffee going out the door. The problem got so bad that the brand switched from getting bags of coffee to buying huge bags of coffee beans that we had to grind on site. They figured that it would be difficult for servers to smuggle out the beans and that not very many people would have grinders at home. We saved so much money when we moved to the beans and stopped getting the pouches of already ground coffee."

This scenario made us wonder how many restaurants are losing bags of coffee to caffeinate the wait staff off-premise. If this form of Product Pinching was a common practice at this popular breakfast chain franchise, wouldn't it be common practice at any restaurant that sells coffee? How many owners are actually keeping track of the bags of coffee versus pots brewed versus cups sold? This interview proved to us that coffee pouches are definitely an area of vulnerability and easy for employees to steal.

Chicago

We spoke extensively with an owner from Chicago who shared his experiences. From this interview, not only did we gain a few horror stories to add to the batch, but also some words of wisdom. The owner first shared a story from when he managed a mall location of a massive, nationwide restaurant chain:

> "One day I'm there with the general manager, and in comes the mall security cop. And he goes, "I saw one of your employees stealing from you." We go out and the cop shows us where the car's at, and in the passenger's floorboard side are these 10-pound chubs of ground beef. And there were like six of 'em. So, 60 pounds of ground beef. Because we were only counting steaks, the employee was stealing ground beef. I had to fire the employee, and it was an emotional thing for me. Somebody you trust, you catch 'em stealing from you and you try to figure out in your mind, like, were they trying to feed their family? But at the end of the day, how do you give grace to somebody that's just blatantly stealing? They didn't steal one chub of ground beef, right? You're gonna feed your family 10 pounds of ground beef? 60 pounds?"

This restaurateur highlighted an important thing to remember when you're dealing with a Product Pincher: they know where your vulnerabilities are and often, they know what you are counting and what you are not counting. A Product Pincher is more likely to steal large quantities of inventory when they know that nobody is consistently monitoring that specific product. He continued:

> "People become entitled; employees become entitled. And what a lot of restaurateurs fail to do is set standards. So one of the ways that a restaurant is most likely to fail is a lack of systems and processes. And today, it's never been easier to go to ChatGPT and say, make me an employee handbook. I mean, the tools that are available today are just obnoxious. Everything's at our fingertips. And by putting something in writing, here is our policy. And balancing food costs with employee benefits, you

get positive results. But, what happens in most situations is, you know, you can have water for free and water turns to Sprite, and Sprite turns to Coke, and then the owner or the manager's like, well, it's just Coke, and they justify it...it's just take an inch. Take an inch, take an inch. A lot of employees will take an inch until you're out of business."

His take on Mid-Shift Munchers was on point. Consuming a product while on the clock becomes common practice and is easily justified in everyone's minds. After all, it's just a Coke. So we asked the owner what technique he found to be best in identifying suspicious behavior among employees:

"Cameras are a must. And you have to watch them. People who are stealing stuff will act differently around the cameras 'cause they'll know where they're at and, you know, they'll keep their back to the cameras. They'll just act stupid around the cameras."

We asked the industry expert what advice he would offer to other restaurateurs or people aspiring to get into the business. His advice could be painful for some to hear but it is relevant and worth sharing:

"Check for shrinkage in high-value inventory items like steak or liquor. Your staff might be taking it home or selling it. Look to see if trash bags are extra heavy or unusually tied off because people might be smuggling stolen products and want to differentiate the bag concealing the good stuff from all the rest of the trash. Make sure the people that are ordering your products are not over-ordering because they could be reselling the product or accepting kickbacks. Audit your employees to see how often mistakes are made. It's really common for a meal to be marked as a kitchen error or customer return just so it can be eaten. Check the to-go boxes when employees are leaving with food to make sure that they rang up what is actually in the box. Do surprise inventory spot checks. It will keep people honest."

It can seem overwhelming, all the extra things an owner-operator has to do to protect themselves. Every suggestion this man shared with us was one we would recommend to anyone reading this book. We asked him, how can a restaurant owner actually enjoy what they do if they have to spend all of their time policing the employees? He was blunt with his answer:

"I was once told that a restaurant owner, second only to a doctor, makes more business-critical decisions per day than any other occupation. And I absolutely believe that. If you don't have somebody that's pouring wisdom into you so that you're able to do things differently, or at least see things differently, this business will suck you in and suck you dry. If you're going into the business because you love to cook, you're a crafts person, not a manager. You shouldn't be an owner. You should work for someone else doing what you're passionate about, not trying to be an owner and managing other people and situations like loss prevention."

Mic drop.

Texas

We interviewed one savvy bar operator who shared with us his own creative way of spotting the Mid-Shift Munchers who were consuming expensive products in his bar. We found his method to be absolutely brilliant:

"We use Red Bull as a mixer for a lot of our drinks at the bar. Every bar in the building is stocked with 8.4-ounce cans of Red Bull, and we count them... but you know that servers and bartenders love to drink that stuff, and we were having a problem managing the theft. I didn't wanna waste a bunch of time chasing around Red Bull thieves. I put a Red Bull machine in the back for the employees, full of 12-ounce cans of Red Bull. If they buy the 8.4-ounce can from the front, it costs them four bucks, but if they buy it from the employee machine in the back, it would only cost them two bucks, and they get more Red Bull in the can. This makes it real easy to spot thieves that steal Red Bull from behind the bar because why would they pay four dollars to get an 8-ounce can when they can pay two dollars and get a 12-ounce can from the back?"

What a smart way to operate! That same operator shared with us a quote that lays it all out:

"It's not a case of if they're gonna steal. Everybody steals. It's just a case of how much you're gonna let them get away with. Every bartender steals to some degree, whether they are overpouring for their friends or giving stuff away or taking cash from the drawer. It's about putting controls in place and making sure they know that you are watching every single move they make."

Massachusetts

Finally, we interviewed a longtime, high-ranking officer from a major nationwide restaurant group that ALL OF US have dined with before. When we asked her about employee theft, she shared some very eye-opening information. Other chapters will feature much of that interview, but one piece of information was specifically relevant to the Inventory Infiltrator.

"I only saw this once, but it probably happens more often than people realize... You know what an Island Oasis machine is? The big drink machines? So the Island Oasis people would give you the machines, and then you'd have to buy the product. They were very happy to give you the machines, and they would manage them and maintain them. And then the restaurant buys the mix from them. Well, the Island Oasis rep came in and was like, "Wait a minute, there were two machines here. Where did the other one go?" And we were like, "No, there weren't. There was only one." And the rep insisted, "No, there were two."

So we decided to dig in and went online to see if we could find the machine. Come to find out that several months prior, there was an eBay listing for an Island Oasis machine posted by one of the bartenders who took the machine! So equipment can go missing and be sold. We lost small wares all the time, like silverware and dishes. So, I mean, you really have to watch everything."

This scenario shocked us. Imagine a bartender smuggling out such a huge piece of equipment and actually getting away with it! It is proof that a thief will take anything that isn't nailed down. They are exceptionally creative and, if the opportunity is there, a thief will take it.

THE PERPETRATOR'S PERSPECTIVE

In our survey, "The Sweethearts" showed up in abundance to share their stories:

> "I worked at a major chain that offered "all you can eat" soup and salad on the menu. I always brought a fresh container of soup "to go" for my customers when I gave them the check. I would tell them that they could eat it for lunch the next day or

as a snack later on, and I always brought them "to go" drinks too. It's how I made good tips." Carol, Orlando, FL

Here's another one....

"I worked at the drive-through of an ice cream shop, and I always gave free ice cream and milkshakes to my girlfriend's family." Dean, Akron, OH

Inventory Infiltration stories were OVERFLOWING our inbox and many of the thieves expressed ZERO GUILT about their prior crimes.

HOW TO PROTECT YOURSELF- YOUR DEFENSE CHECKLIST

Here is a checklist of solutions to guard yourself against Inventory Infiltrators. In a business like yours, where margins are razor thin, you cannot afford to disregard these important controls:

- **Biometric manager access** uses fingerprint technology to prevent employees from using manager codes to perform comps and voids. Security levels that restrict lower-level employees from doing comps and voids are a necessity.
- **POS & surveillance** is the only way to capture everything going on in the business. Cameras around dumpsters, inside walk-ins, cameras on every door, on break areas, on the line, behind the bar and on every POS terminal will provide the evidence necessary to bust an Inventory Infiltrator. Text overlay with POS transactions recorded on the surveillance footage can show what items are actually

being rung up versus what is being served to customers.
- **Auditing software** that marries the data from your POS with surveillance footage can identify suspicious activities within your business. This technology will save you hours of time in auditing and is very affordable compared to hiring a full-time loss prevention employee.
- **Inventory procedures** can make or break you so make sure you are separating responsibilities between different employees. In other words, the person counting the inventory when it is received should not be the person who orders it. The person responsible for counting at the beginning of a shift should be someone different than the one performing end of day counts.
- **Audit** employee sales and transactions to make sure everyone is in line. A Basic Bandit and a Sweetheart will stick out like a sore thumb when you consistently audit sales and POS activity.
- **Policies and procedures** that are clearly communicated to your employees around their consumption, discounts and "the rules" will make your standards clear to the staff and will set a zero-tolerance for Inventory Infiltration.
    - **Offer rewards** to employees who report suspicious activities
    - **Employee meals** should be heavily audited and discounts performed by senior management
    - **Loyalty programs** should not be available for employees to use. Instead, offer rewards to your staff for enrolling guests in loyalty programs.
    - **Providing a "Family Meal"** can prevent mid-shift munching while showing your employees that you

care, creating a better culture. Before opening each day, offer a meal to your staff that is the same for everyone and use it as an opportunity to educate your team on your food, how it tastes and how to sell it to the guests.

- **Ring up EVERYTHING** and comp it out. Even if you choose to give sodas to your staff while they are working, make it a practice to ring the items up and comp them out so you can take advantage of tax benefits, and properly track your goods.
- **Offer resignation** as an option to any thieves you catch. Giving an employee the ability to leave on their own terms is often an attractive option to someone who has been caught being dishonest.
- **Provide a Handbook** that clearly outlines all the rules and defines your standards. Get your employees to sign the handbook or a document that states that they have read and understand the handbook. Set a zero-tolerance policy for theft and make sure that your employees understand every activity that is considered theft so there are no situations where employees innocently assume that consuming your product is a perk of the job.
- **Check references and backgrounds** so that you can avoid hiring repeat offenders or professional scammers.
- **Do bag checks** if employees must bring their bags into the building. A better solution is setting a rule that prevents personal bags from being brought into work.
- **Implement a buddy system** when employees go to their cars at the end of a shift, setting the precedent that a manager may escort you to your vehicle.

This has an added benefit of ensuring employee safety.
- **No car visits** during breaks. Employees should not go to their vehicles during a shift. Require your employees to park away from the dumpster.

SIGNS OF THE INVENTORY INFILTRATOR

The warning signs for Inventory Infiltration may seem self-explanatory after reading this chapter, but we wanted to tie them all together in a list of red flags to help you spot these crafty crooks. Start paying closer attention and taking note when you recognize these characteristics in your crew and ensure the policies, standards and procedures you have in place are sufficient to stop the inventory bleeding immediately.

$ **Inventory Infiltrators** memorize manager access codes, or hold one themselves and are often highly trusted members of the team.

$ **Inventory Infiltrators** may be savvy on operating technology solutions.

$ **Inventory Infiltrators** like to carry bags and backpacks in and out of the building where they can conceal product.

$ **Inventory Infiltrators** may frequently "forget" to ring up chargeable beverages and may often make "to go" drinks for their customers.

$ **Inventory Infiltrators** may maintain inventory counts and relationships with Vendors.

$ **Inventory Infiltrators** may cook a bunch of food close to closing time so they can take it home and "not waste it" or may often be spotted chewing food in the kitchen.

$ **Inventory Infiltrators** are often beloved team members who hand out bar drinks, apps and desserts to colleagues and friends.

$ **Inventory Infiltrators** can be any age or gender, but Sweethearts are often teenagers who are giving away products to friends to gain popularity so look for people who often have friends or family visiting them at work.

$ **Inventory Infiltrators** may act suspiciously around cameras such as looking at the cameras or turning their backs to the cameras or avoiding them. They may focus on surveillance monitors in the office to learn where the cameras are and what they cover.

$ **Inventory Infiltrators** are often responsible for taking out the trash, or they may visit their vehicles during the shift to stash products they have stolen.

$ **Inventory Infiltrators** may work in teams to accomplish their goals. It is not uncommon for Snakes to operate as Inventory Infiltrators, enabling lower-level employees to steal as well.

FOOD FOR THOUGHT

One bit of advice that the high-ranking officer (who busted the drink machine thief) shared stuck out as valuable information. When asked how to create an environment that was NOT conducive to theft, she said:

> "It is my personal feeling that when you incentivize people to do the right thing versus having to catch them or punish them for doing the wrong thing, you end up farther ahead."

This struck us as sound advice on how to look at the big picture of preventing theft in your restaurant. It doesn't mean that people will not steal from you or try to take advantage of you. It *suggests* that when you build your **processes, standards and controls** around *rewarding good behavior,* Inventory Infiltration and the other types of theft discussed in this book can be drastically decreased.

THE FINAL DISH ON "INVENTORY INFILTRATORS"

Inventory Infiltrators are never going away. They are not a problem you can solve and move on from. As long as you are operating, Inventory Infiltration will be a viable threat to your livelihood and your survival.

What is important to remember is that **every single ingredient housed in your restaurant <u>belongs to you.</u>** Every ingredient <u>costs you money</u>. **SO TAKE OWNERSHIP!** You establish the rules for your staff regarding what is acceptable and what is not. Managing this threat requires full-time diligence, but the way you lead your team will keep a tight lid on what they can get away with. Inventory Infiltration happens right before your eyes so keep your head on a swivel and **BE VIGILANT.**

CHAPTER 6
THE SNAKE

It's time to introduce you to the most nefarious threat to your business: **The Snake.**

Remember, at Jack and Jill's when Don, the kitchen manager, took the tenderloin? He was a Snake, operating as a Product Pincher. Remember Sean, the manager? He took cash and was a Snake behaving as a blatant Cash Stasher, a villain that we will expand upon further, later on in this book. He also comped out sales for Mike on the POS system, being the cool guy and snaking around as a Basic Bandit. Two of the three managers working the shift that day took Jack and Jill for hundreds of dollars. If that happens consistently, it adds up to tens of thousands of dollars a year in theft at the Gastropub.

WHAT IF YOU HAVE A SNAKE IN YOUR HOUSE?!??

Think about it: The nature of "The Snake." We aren't talking about the helpful garden snake that cleans out other pests. The snakes we are dealing with are highly venomous and aggressive in their actions.

Imagine that you literally have a venomous snake in your house. They slink around undetected, slithering behind your furniture, curling up under your bed while you sleep and navigating through your domain, completely unseen. You believe you're safe. You have no idea you have such a dangerous creature in your house. A snake can move so stealthily and quietly that you won't even know that there's been one lurking around until months later when it sheds its skin and you find the remains or even worse, when the snake bites you. Maybe it's not 100% venomous- and maybe it even felt justified biting you and was just protecting itself but, either way, you are suffering pain and trauma, once bitten.

Don't leave *your* door open and allow these sneaky, unwanted creatures to enter and roam freely throughout *your* castle.

THE UNCOMFORTABLE TRUTH

In our survey, we confirmed our belief that **the people you trust the most are your biggest threat for internal theft within your operation.** But, even approaching the survey with this pre-existing hypothesis, the actual data **still** blew our freaking minds!

From the mouths of the thieves and victims alike, the survey showed that 83% of the crimes committed within bars and restaurants are perpetrated by **THE MOST TRUSTED** employees on the payroll.

83% of the criminals, no matter what types of theft they are committing, are actually "Snakes!"

It makes you sick to your stomach. Not only do Snakes harm your business, they add a layer of emotional betrayal to the mix so you get not only a blow to your wallet but also to your heart.

NEWSWORTHY

The news is rife with stories of snakelike behavior in the hospitality industry. Throughout this book, Snakes are easily identifiable, committing different thefts, and presenting themselves in a variety of ways. Highly adaptable, the Snake will slither into any opportunity it encounters in order to steal from you.

Texas

In a popular TV series, Mystery Diners, that aired from 2011 to 2016, one episode titled "Menu Mayhem" revealed that a chef was stealing products and ingredients from the restaurant and using his labor time to prepare food for his secret, competing catering business. Who on earth would have ever thought of this scheme?!?!

The Snake navigated as a Crooked Clocker, stealing time, as well as a Product Pincher, stealing ingredients. He worked a second job while on the clock, prepping the product and taking it out the door. This Snake was even taking orders and payments for his catering hustle while he was operating as the chef for the business featured in the show's episode. The side hustle didn't just belong to the chef, but another manager was also involved in the scheme. This episode showed us that Snakes will cover for each other and clearly can operate easier if they can work as a team.[1]

New York

The New York Post published a story in April 2024 about an alarming Snake tale. For over a decade, the Italian Hospitality Empire, Cipriani, alleged that they suffered theft from high-level

Snakes working with a Villainous Vendor, a character we will introduce later on in this book. The business alleged that their Operations Director approved false, inflated and duplicate invoices worth an estimated $5 million from one of their hardware vendors. According to a lawsuit filed in Manhattan Supreme Court, Cipriani provided evidence that the Operations Director took a cut of these false invoices for himself.

In addition, both the President and General Manager allegedly created a shell company to defraud Cipriani for services like fridge maintenance, etc. They apparently issued bogus invoices for YEARS with the Facilities Manager allegedly helping by placing and picking up orders to make it look like the company received all the invoiced products and services. These Snakes even used the corporate credit card to purchase AirPods, fleece sweaters and a diamond ring. The multiple alleged thefts took the company for MILLIONS.[2]

As of our book's publication deadline, this case is still ongoing in Manhattan Court. Imagine the court fees involved!

California

The Los Angeles Times reported a California case from December 2023, in which a partner was accused of using company funds to open other restaurants without the other owners' knowledge or consent. In the lawsuit, the partner alleged that her son, who was also her business partner, used money from their shared Silver Lake restaurant (El Cochinito) to fund another concept, Café Tropical and to open another one, Bolita, without authority or consent from the other partners. The original family restaurant had been open for over 50 years and ended up closing, likely because of the dispute.

According to the article, "A letter from the Mother's lawyer to her son in April 2022 stated that the son, along with a business partner, who was also a defendant in the lawsuit, had to account for $2.5 million that had either been spent or transferred from company to company. The parties agreed to a settlement in May 2023 in which the son would pay his mother $350,000 and in exchange, she and his sister would transfer their stock in the company to the son," according to court documents. At the time of publication of the LA Times article, "the son had already missed the July payment date."[3]

It's funny how sometimes the people you'd take a bullet for are the ones behind the trigger.

WORD ON THE STREET

We reached out to hospitality owners and managers to get their "Hard Takes on The Snakes." Wrap your brain around these insane situations!!

The Nightclub & Event Venue

First, we interviewed a longtime General Manager for one of the largest privately-owned nightclubs and event venues in the US. When we asked him if he had ever had a Snake in his house, he shared some interesting stories:

> "One day our T-shirt vendor came in with a check for our Gift Shop Manager, who was on vacation at the time. We asked the vendor what the check was for, and the vendor told us that it was the gift shop manager's share of the T-shirt sales. That was how we discovered that a portion of our profits were being

given as a kickback to one of our trusted managers. We set up a sting and caught him, fired him, and perp-walked him through the club. We found that a lot of vendors are keen on offering kickbacks, bonuses or perks to our managers for ordering their products. We have a strict policy in place that kickbacks of any form are not allowed. We can't have our liquor manager getting free bottles of booze from the liquor vendor, and we can't have our kitchen manager getting free vacations from the food vendors. All of those perks belong to the owner, and it's their decision if they want to distribute them as rewards to the employees or if they wanna keep them for themselves."

The hits kept coming...

"We had a kitchen manager one time, and his wife also worked in the kitchen and they worked together as a team to steal food. The dude put it right down his pants and walked out the door with it on multiple occasions. Crazy amounts of food- pounds of ground beef, whole salmon, steaks, you name it. We caught him on surveillance eventually because we have over 100 cameras and audit them regularly but we had been busy focusing our attention on auditing bartenders and we trusted our kitchen staff so we weren't spending a lot of time looking at that stuff... so they got away with it for a little while. When we did catch it, we fired them both and perp-walked them but it was painful for us because we had come to really rely on them, and we trusted them to manage the kitchen aspect of our operation."

The Ohio Bar & Restaurant

Next, we visited with a former bar and restaurant owner from Ohio who was not always present because he had a part-time career as a professional athlete in Europe. It saddened us to hear the stories of how the former owner's most trusted employees and friends took advantage of him. This man ended up losing his million-dollar investment and eventually had to close the doors. He largely attributed the loss of his longtime restaurant dream to internal theft. Some of the Snake tales that this man shared with us were truly appalling:

> "I found out my best friend was showing up at the bar and literally walking in the back door in the middle of a shift, going into the cooler and stealing a case of beer and walking out. He didn't think anything of it. Other friends would come in and drink and just tell my bartenders to put their bills on my tab. It put me in an awful position with people I cared about."

He continued:

> "I fired people for theft left and right, everything you can imagine. I caught them and I fired them. I had a great POS system in place, and I had cameras in place. But then they would file for unemployment, and I would miss my dispute window because I was overseas, and they would get it. It was literally the money I had to pay in unemployment and taxes and stuff that became so astronomical that I believe it finally put me out of business. I mean all the theft I was catching was affecting my bottom line, and then I fired so many thieves that I couldn't keep up with the disputes. Sometimes I didn't even know they were happening because I was out of the country."

The Bakery Chain

We also interviewed an independent entrepreneur who founded a cupcake concept that she grew to five locations within her home state. This lady shared with us the most heartbreaking interview as she was completely blindsided by the Snake in her house:

"I was in quite a bit of denial that I had a problem. My dad had just died. I leaned on my assistant heavily at that time because I had just opened up a new store. I was incredibly busy, and I gave her freedoms that I would not have typically given to somebody. I would say grab the deposit from whichever store it was and use that money to go to the store and get the things that we need and then take it back to the other store. She was kind of filling in [for] the things that I used to do.

You know, looking back, that's clearly what started all of this... I started noticing that I wasn't paying attention and I was trusting her way too much and just giving her free rein and trust because I was dealing with my dad dying, and so she had the opportunity. And she took it. I just kind of dismissed it and let it go on for goodness, eight months, nine months? Before I started to really, you know, realize what was going on and pay attention."

The scam that her Snake was running was elaborate. The assistant actually opened another account at the same bank as the owner's account, and she would divert cash to her account when she went to deposit the restaurant's cash on behalf of the owner. She would steal cash from the bag and say it was going for supply purchases, and then not purchase the supplies and keep the cash.

The owner ended up auditing her assistant, and **she eventually stopped counting when she reached the $30,000 mark in theft.** *This number did not include the theft of customer credit card numbers.* The owner described the auditing experience as "stomach-turning" and said it made her "too physically ill to continue the audit" once she got to $30k. The owner established that the theft had been going on for a minimum of eight months, and so she reached out to the police. Unfortunately, because all of her locations were in different jurisdictions, she would have had to invest tens of thousands of dollars for a forensic accountant to audit the books and prove the crimes to prosecute the assistant. Because most of the crime happened away from surveillance cameras and the owner had given her assistant permission to make deposits, it was going to be a lengthy battle. The owner opted to confront the assistant, and she videotaped the conversation.

The Snake never fully confessed to her crimes, but as soon as the conversation ended, the Snake went home, packed up everything she owned and immediately moved across the country. She walked out on her lease and her entire life to avoid the consequences for the crimes she had committed. The owner ended up selling the concept and getting out of the cupcake business with such a bad taste in her mouth that she could never trust another employee again. She has since opened three new concepts: an event venue where she can control all cash and product, a meal delivery service where she can control all cash and product, and a food truck that she operates by herself.

Wounds heal and scars fade, but the snakebite that this entrepreneur suffered was so traumatizing that it forever changed her belief in people and her ability to trust others.

Absolutely heartbreaking.

THE PERPETRATOR'S PERSPECTIVE

In our survey, one person shared a scenario that is likely a common motive among the Snakes:

> "We had a family restaurant with my older brothers and my dad. When I started out, I was the cashier. I was sixteen and ran the cash register, and they taught me how to do it all. For a couple of years, they would have me set aside cash tickets and not ring them up. They were using the money for dope, but I

didn't realize that at the time because I was still kind of a kid. Later on, when I started partying with them, I used the same scam to be able to pay for my own stuff. It was a cycle, and it became generational at our restaurant. We ended up going out of business because we were drug addicts and we were using the business to fund it. We were all hiding it from each other, too. We're all sober now, but it sucks. We had to lose everything and can't get our restaurant back because we were so stupid," Jennifer, Shreveport, LA

HOW TO PROTECT YOURSELF- YOUR DEFENSE CHECKLIST

- **Access logs** that track when employees use high security clearance to perform comps, voids and no sales are essential for auditing your staff.
- **Surveillance** is not optional, especially if you are not at the business. You cannot have enough surveillance in your operation. Make sure that you maintain the access to surveillance data and that no other employees can delete or manipulate the footage. You should regularly check your system to ensure that specific cameras have not been moved or disabled.
- **Staying involved** will serve as a theft deterrent and will show the crew that you are tracking and watching everything. A "Snake" won't feel comfortable under a spotlight, so ensure you make every significant business decision and that you approve all purchases and partnerships.
- **Regularly audit** your point-of-sale and surveillance data. Using technology to marry the data from the two solutions can identify theft without loss prevention becoming a full-time job for you.

- **Maintain control** and do not let the inmates run the asylum. Do not allow yourself to become overly friendly with your staff or pass high-level responsibilities to employees who display charm and charisma.
- **Invest in technology** like biometrics, point-of-sale, surveillance, and loss prevention analysis technology. They are all "must-haves" if you want to protect yourself properly from Snakes.
- **Offer rewards** to your employees for reporting suspicious behavior or activities that they witness or hear about.
- **Maintain transparency** by communicating to your staff and partners that you are aware of the genuine threat of internal theft and that you are proactively monitoring the business <u>at all times</u>. Establish a zero-tolerance policy for theft.
- **Require dual signatures** so that there is accountability when money is spent amongst partners and check-signing employees.
- **Do background checks** to make sure that the managers and team members you are hiring have not gotten into trouble for theft in previous jobs. Check their references.
- **Use a third-party bookkeeping company** so that you have additional oversight besides yourself.
- **Have formal partnership agreements with exit clauses and clear roles,** making sure that you eliminate loopholes and identify financial boundaries, reporting rules, buyout clauses and clear exit plans in case of future disputes or transitions with your partners.
- **Policies and procedures** that are clearly communicated to your employees will protect you

from having to pay unemployment when you discover theft and need to terminate an employee. Document everything. Distribute employee handbooks and get signatures for receipt from your employees, acknowledging that they understand the rules.

- **Inventory ordering** should be managed by more than one individual and should be separate from inventory counting and/or receiving inventory from vendors.
- **Inventory counting** should be rotated between different employees to make sure that the person who counts the inventory is not responsible for end-of-day counts.
- **Vendor communication** is vital to ensure that your employees do not have better relationships with your vendors than you do. Make sure that you clearly explain to your vendors that you do not allow your employees to accept kickbacks and that if you find out that kickbacks are going on, you will find a new vendor to meet your needs.
- **Rotate responsibilities** to prevent one person from controlling too much.

SIGNS OF THE SNAKE

The woman who owned the cupcake chain shared that there were red flags that she ignored. Her personal life had become so heavy that she didn't have time to follow up when her gut instinct was telling her to look a little closer at her assistant. Most people who have had a Snake in their house would say the same.

Here are some signs to watch for to spot the sneaky Snakes you may have. Use discernment when hiring and remember these characteristics when you are looking for your next trusted employee or partner:

$ **A Snake** is someone who may work very, very hard to gain your trust or repeatedly emphasizes how much you can trust them and often asks for more access and responsibility.

$ **A Snake** holds more responsibility than other employees and is usually filling valuable roles in the operation, such as: *your business partner, your best friend, your manager, your favorite employee, your employee trainer, your family member or even your spouse.*

$ **A Snake** holds the highest levels of security within your business systems and often has keys to the building, your office and alarm codes.

$ **A Snake** is given access to handle cash.

$ **A Snake** often has access to credit card data.

$ **A Snake** is often categorized as a hard worker or "hustler."

$ **A Snake** may have extreme financial pressures within their personal lives.

$ **A Snake** may like to "live large" outside of work.

$ **A Snake** likely has a very good understanding of how the technology works within your operation, maybe even better than you do.

$ **A Snake** might be responsible for ordering products and maintaining inventory counts and vendor relationships.

$ **A Snake** is often inclined to maintain complete control of their job responsibilities, and he or she does not want anyone else to get a peek at their work because they fear discovery.

$ **A Snake** may have personal relationships or friendships with people at lower levels of your operation and/or is very popular with the crew.

$ **A Snake** may handle bank deposits, and they often have access to the safe.

$ **A Snake** may handle cash purchases for supplies outside of your normal vendor relationships.

$ **A Snake** may know more than you about the goings-on in your operation.

$ **A Snake** will use every form of theft that we discuss in this book. For a Snake, nothing is off-limits.

$ **A Snake** likely has many years of experience in the industry and may brag about their expertise so that you will trust them with more responsibility which will give them greater access to your money and products.

$ **A Snake** might exhibit an air of ownership over the operation.

$ **A Snake** may work in teams with others to commit theft and fraud.

$ **A Snake** may display a sense of entitlement.

$ **A Snake** may be disgruntled about their current rate of pay or status within the operation, desiring or needing more.

$ **A Snake** may be a drug addict or alcoholic.

FOOD FOR THOUGHT

In the dozens of interviews we had with Hospitality Consultants across the country, they all shared a common experience: whenever they try to warn an independent restaurateur about the threat of internal theft, the client will always say that they *"trust their employees."* It is common to hear the response, *"I don't have to worry about that because I've got my family working here with me."* We learned it is usually VERY offensive to restaurant clients for a Hospitality Consultant to even suggest that a friend or loved one might steal from the business. The truth not only hurts, but ignoring it could cost you thousands of dollars and even your entire business.

THE FINAL DISH ON "THE SNAKE"

We are gonna say it again. **The data is clear: three out of four of your employees are going to steal from you at some point.**

While the other types of thieves will hurt your business, a Snake can devastate it.

Part of the reason a Snake is so devastating is that, according to the Association of Certified Fraud Examiners (ACFE), these kinds of snaky schemes typically **last longer than 24 months before they're detected**. Another reason, again according to the ACFE's 2024 report, a partner or family member's theft or fraud causes losses of $400,000 or more before discovery.[4] This was the highest damage amount in any category that was examined in the report. *Just imagine how much damage a Snake could do in your business if their thieving ways weren't discovered for over two years?*

Marinate on that.

CHAPTER 7
CASH STASHER

Now, we are going to have a chat about another kind of villain that you will probably face in your hospitality career: **The Cash Stasher.**

At Jack and Jill's Gastropub, Sean, the Snaky Manager, stashed cash in his pocket from the safe. Darren, the bartender, stashed cash in his pocket when he counted his drawer and found that it was over by five dollars. These two sloppy stashers didn't think twice about pilfering cash when given the opportunity.

While many thieves will use elaborate schemes, a Cash Stasher doesn't hesitate to engage in a typical grab-and-go whenever they can. This doesn't mean that they aren't elaborate schemers, however. Sometimes, they will embezzle money through fake employee paychecks using ghost employee personas that they have concocted out of thin air. *How's that for creative heisting?!* A Cash Stasher may even make up fake invoices to fake vendors to pay themselves the cash. A Cash Stasher will also take money out of the drawer to pay for supplies that they never actually buy.

WHAT IF YOU HAVE A CASH STASHER WORKING FOR YOU?

Do Cash Stashers run away after they rob you, like bank robbers do? Unfortunately, the answer is often no. These thieving parasites have found a host in you and your establishment, and they will feed and feed until there is nothing left to feed on. Having a Cash Stasher on your payroll guarantees they will cost you a fortune.

A Cash Stasher will skim from the register by taking small amounts of cash from the drawer and altering records to hide it. They will "tap the till" and remove cash before a deposit is made. Cash Stashers will hit the "no sale" button and pocket cash without recording a transaction. They even have the guts to go right to the safe and, if they have access, they will maneuver like cat burglars and steal everything they can get their hands on. A stealthy Cash Stasher could even wire funds out of the company account to their own private stash account, and if nobody's watching? They get away with it.

This begs the question: would you ask an employee to hold your wallet for a few weeks? Or, would you leave your ATM card on the bar and "trust" that nobody steals the number? *Of course not.* But if you did, you would check your bank account regularly to make sure nobody did anything shady to you. So why is your restaurant any different? Why blindly trust your employees when they have constant access to your money? Because they work for you? Because you are friends with them? Because they're your family?

It's sad, but these schemes often go unnoticed for months or even years, especially when the owner trusts their staff and does minimal to no auditing. Sometimes, the crooks get away with their crimes because the owner doesn't notice the theft.

As we've said repeatedly in this book, it doesn't matter how close you are with people. It doesn't matter how much you trust them or if you come from the same family gene pool or if you grew up together. Those relationships will often NOT prevent someone from stealing when the opportunity presents itself. Cold, hard cash is tempting and in a bar or restaurant, it's everywhere.

THE UNCOMFORTABLE TRUTH

In our own nationwide survey, 44% of our respondents admitted to stealing cash from their hospitality jobs. Glenn Withiam, the Executive Editor at Cornell University, *also* conducted a study on employee theft in restaurants. His data was **JUST AS DAMNING** as ours. He found that 48% of the respondents admitted to taking over $500 worth of cash or merchandise from the restaurants and bars where they worked.[1] This means that you can hang your hat on the fact that a large percentage of your employees are going to steal cash from you.

Olin Business School analyzed 83,153 restaurant waiters across 1,049 United States restaurants.

Damn, what a survey!!! Very impressive!!! Anyway, we digress...

The study showed that till and transaction manipulation is a widespread problem that DROPS with tighter oversight.[2] It means that cash exposure is REAL, but it also means that it is PREVENTABLE.

Think about it; it's your wallet, right? It's your check card sitting on the bar. IT'S YOUR MONEY!!! YOU control who touches it, when they touch it, and who is watching them touch it. To protect yourself, employees who handle your cash should **ALWAYS** feel like they are being watched. If you agree with this, it is up to **YOU** to create that vibe. We will show you how!

NEWSWORTHY

We found some **CRAZY** Cash Stasher stories that made the news. Remember, these are stories where someone was successful in catching the thieves. *Imagine how many times Cash Stashers actually get away with their crimes!* And also, take note: more often than not, a Snake was involved in the heists. See for yourself:

Florida

Fox 13 News in Tampa Bay reported on a Cash Stasher in April 2025. Police arrested the general manager of the Oak & Stone Restaurant in Bradenton, Florida, after he tried to pull off an old-fashioned safe heist. The general manager arrived in the early morning hours sporting a ski mask, unlocked the door and deactivated the cameras. He then forced open the safe and cash registers. He wiped everything down to avoid leaving fingerprints but wasn't considering that other surveillance cameras near the property could catch him committing the crime. The Cash Stasher made off with approximately $3500 in his burglary gone wrong.[3]

Georgia

WCTV aired a story of four sloppy Cash Stashers out of Thomas County, Georgia, in June 2025. The thieves were employees (one of them a manager) of the local IHOP, and they had quite a scheme running: they failed to deposit 8K in cash to the bank and also stole 13K in tip money! IHOP fired all four of the Cash Stashers, and now they face felony theft charges.[4]

Tennessee

WBIR ran a story on July 4, 2025, about a MASSIVE Cash Stash. An employee of a popular restaurant in Knoxville, Chuy's, stole almost 28K from the business. On eighteen occasions, the employee kept cash store deposits instead of taking them to the bank. He pretended to make the deposits, logging them into the company's computerized funds management system as being "paid" even though he was stashing the cash. The shortage was discovered when auditors compared the deposit amounts that were logged in the system with the actual bank deposit history. When management confronted him, the Cash Stasher admitted to taking the money and said he had used it to move into a new place and buy new furniture and clothes. The Cash Stasher said he "did not realize how large the amount had become."[5]

Australia

In Queensland, Australia, news.com.au reported on a Cash Stashing theft that went WAY left....

In May 2024, an ex-employee of a local cafe used a copied key to sneak into the business. The Cash Stasher took $2500 over a two-week spree of secret visits to the cafe.

The cafe owners took matters into their own hands. They ABDUCTED THE THIEF, CABLE TIED HIM, CUT HIS HAIR, TORTURED HIM and demanded he repay them what he had stolen. THEN they called the Cash Stasher's mother and told her they had kidnapped her son and demanded she give them the money he had stolen. The cafe owners were upstanding members of the community, but apparently, they were triggered by the theft and they responded in THE WRONG WAY.

Because the cafe owners abducted the thief, they turned him into a VICTIM, and they ruined their chances of getting true justice. They got their money back from the mom and then released their prisoner in a public park, but they ended up in court themselves facing kidnapping charges because of the whacked-out "loss recovery techniques" they used.[6]

Let this story be a lesson that, if you *DO* catch someone stealing, **please, please, involve the police**. Do not cable-tie the thief. Do not cut their hair. Do not torture them or hold them for ransom. No matter how tempting it is to take matters into your own hands, letting the police handle it is <u>always</u> the better way.

WORD ON THE STREET

In our conversations with various industry experts, we heard some interesting stories about Cash Stashers. One restaurant owner learned the hard way that sometimes the sweetest employees are really "wolves in sheep's clothing."

The Pensacola Beach, FL Restaurant

"Every Monday, we tally the weekend's cash earnings at our restaurant. One time, I noticed the numbers were messed up. What we counted wasn't what I was going to deposit. At first, it was small. $20 here, $50 there. But by the third week, $300 was missing. The safe was locked, and the cameras showed no break-ins. Only three people had access to the money: myself, my chef and my hostess. The hostess had been working for me for two months, and she was bright, charming, and always eager to work overtime. The customers loved her, but my gut was screaming at me. Sure enough, the hostess was stealing cash when she would lock up the gift cards in the safe. I felt so stupid for giving a complete stranger access to my safe."

This owner was clearly allowing the wrong people to have access to the money. She was watching surveillance cameras and locking the safe but never considered that a hostess with a two-month job tenure could be a risk. Not everyone knows how to "think like a thief." The sweet, older lady who told us this story would never have imagined that a thief could be the innocent little hostess she had recently hired.

The lesson? **TRUST NOBODY.**

The Ohio Bar & Restaurant

"At one point, the safe got robbed in the office. I know it was one of my managers that did it because they came in through the ceiling tiles, all Mission-Impossible like, and they knew exactly how to get to the safe through the ceiling and avoid the security cameras in the office. Only my managers would've known how to do that and not get caught on camera. Whoever it was came in through the ceiling, took a blowtorch to the safe and took me for three grand."

This situation is so frustrating because nobody ever got caught. The owner knew it was one of their managers behind the crime but could do nothing to prove it. We imagine that more times than not, this is the case with Cash Stashers. The best ones will move from location to location, never staying in one place for too long. Just like bank robbers.

THE PERPETRATOR'S PERSPECTIVE

Now, let's go back to our survey on theft in the hospitality industry to see what a self-admitted thief had to say about the fine art of Cash Stashing:

> "I was a bartender at a small bar. When customers paid in cash, I pocketed the cash. Sometimes, I entered a lower-priced product into the cash register and kept the change. Sometimes, I didn't ring anything up. I just poured. One day, I was in the process of doing one when my boss walked up behind me and saw me. I guess he'd been paying attention for awhile... anyway, I was fired on the spot." William, Dallas TX

This bartender was doing a very common thing in the industry, which is why it is so important to have surveillance with POS-integrated text overlay.

Here's another bartender story and you will notice in hers that she learned from other employees how to rip off the bar where she worked:

> "I was a bartender for a few weeks at a country bar. They only had cash registers. When I got hired, the other bartenders taught me that if the tips were shitty, we just took the cash and didn't ring up the order. The woman that owned the bar didn't have surveillance or anything so we were able to get a bunch during the shift. Most nights, each of us made an extra 80 bucks in tips by not ringing stuff up. The owner was never even there..."
> Amanda, Ormond Beach, FL

One more to share and this one is a family affair. We wonder how the story ended...

"I caught my sister stealing cash out of the register at our family bar to give to her boyfriend for blow (cocaine). I was running the cash register that night, and if I hadn't seen her do it, the drawer would've been short and it would've looked like I took the money." Kate, Lewisville, TX

Admittedly, in our survey, nobody admitted to Cash-Stashing scams worth thousands of dollars. The survey was not completely anonymous, and nobody was willing to confess their prior, possibly large, cash crimes. But there were many stories similar to the ones above.

Cash Stashing is a common crime in the hospitality industry. The amounts may be small and happen over a period of time, so they will go unnoticed. Sometimes the amounts are large and happen in one instance. Either way, every time it happens, **IT IS YOUR MONEY!**

HOW TO PROTECT YOURSELF- YOUR DEFENSE CHECKLIST

Check out this "must have" list of solutions that you can use to guard yourself against the notorious Cash Stasher. Remember that cash theft is preventable in your business! Use this checklist to make sure you are adequately covering your butt!

- **Dual custody** should be required for cash deposits and banking.
- **Invest in technology** like POS, loss prevention auditing technology and cameras.
    - **Surveillance cameras** should be everywhere without exception. Don't skimp on placement! Thirty-six cameras minimum for an average-sized restaurant. Use a third-party data auditing solution to catch things you might miss.

- **Randomly audit** POS transactions, deleted orders, no sales and payroll.
- **Cross-check reimbursements** with support documentation.
- **Audit** your employee rosters. Make sure that the people you are paying to work are REAL human beings!
- **Watch your bank account** and make yourself aware of how every penny is spent.
- **Manage access to your accounts.** Don't let employees or vendors access them.
- **Policies and procedures** should be clearly communicated to your employees regarding cash handling.
    - **Rotate responsibility** for cash handling.
    - **Require two people** to count drawers
    - **Safe access** should only happen with you present but if it must be accessed while you are not present, safe access should run on the buddy system. Use a safe that alerts you when someone opens it and watch surveillance to monitor it.
    - **Access** to the building should not be permitted after hours.
    - **Cash supply runs** should require a photo of the receipt and a photo of the goods emailed to you if you can't verify the supplies in person.
    - **Employee files** should include a photo of the employee at your restaurant and a copy of their driver's license before they start.

SIGNS OF THE CASH STASHER

People often say, *"I should've known because all the signs were there,"* after they realize that a criminal has taken them for a ride.

Pause for a moment to review the following points and consider the people that work for you today:

$ **Cash Stashers** may have financial stress or exhibit entitlement. They may frequently complain about their pay and suggest that they deserve more.

$ **Cash Stashers** may have new, expensive items that are not in line with their income. They may drive a fancy new car, always wear new clothes or go on extra extravagant vacations.

$ **Cash Stashers** may buy food or drinks for their coworkers or excessively pay tabs for other people. This is how they buy silence.

$ **Cash Stashers** may get defensive when questioned about drawer balances, comps, or voids. They prefer to count the money in isolation.

$ **Cash Stashers** often have control issues and insist on anything to do with cash handling being done by themselves. They will be resistant to cross-training or rotation of cash duties.

$ **Cash Stashers** don't want other people covering their shifts or their drawer. This could expose discrepancies.

$ **Cash Stashers** may be responsible for making cash deposits into your account.

$ **Cash Stashers** may be responsible for hiring employees and running the payroll. These people could create ghost employees and pay them while actually diverting that pay to their own accounts.

$ **Cash Stashers** may conveniently "lose" deposit slips, cash reports, register tapes, etc.

$ **Cash Stashers** may be responsible for using cash to pay vendors or going to the store to get supplies for the business.

$ **Cash Stashers** may be responsible for emptying vending machines, jukeboxes, arcade games, or pool tables that are within your establishment.

$ **Cash Stashers** may work in teams or teach others how to steal. This behavior serves as an insurance policy that protects them from being ratted out.

FOOD FOR THOUGHT

To change things up a bit, we thought we would give you a little hope. Not all people are bad guys. Not everyone is going to steal from you without remorse. Enjoy this heartwarming tale of one Cash Stasher who turned honest:

> The inventor of the chimichanga, the famous restaurateur and owner of The El Charro Cafe, had Cash Stashers operating in her restaurant. She was completely unaware of the criminals or the crimes that they committed against her. In 2018, CBS featured a story about the restaurant owner from Tucson, Arizona, who received an anonymous letter in the mail. The letter was inside an envelope that was also stuffed with $1000 in cash. Side note: The 72-year-old restaurant owner had been mugged at the grocery store the day before she received the letter and the cash. The timing of the anonymous message couldn't have been more perfect.
>
> The letter read: "I worked for you as a waitress very briefly back in the 1990s. One of the waiters I worked with had encouraged me to 'forget' to ring in a few drinks each shift and pocket the cash. And for some stupid reason, I did." The former server asked the owner to accept the anonymous apology and repayment plus 20 years of interest. The sender explained that she had grown up in the church and knew better than to steal. She said, "It's been 20 years, but I still carry remorse."[7]

However, all's-well-that-ends-well stories like this one are rare. So, do not wait around for thieves to one day send you envelopes full of cash with anonymous confessions and apologies. Protect yourself today!

THE FINAL DISH ON "CASH STASHERS"

Cash Stashers are one of the most common and harmful villains you will face as a hospitality owner. The magnitude of their crimes is jaw-dropping. We hope that this chapter has given you a newfound motivation for asserting yourself and controlling what happens with your cash. If you think that the scenarios we have described could not or would not happen to you, we hope it's because you ALREADY have the controls in place to protect yourself. *Remember, surveillance is not optional.*

The key takeaway is that oversight prevents Cash Stashing. So pay attention!!! Delegating any responsibilities involving cash handling could spell financial disaster for you and your business. If you currently have other people managing specific tasks centered on cash, it's time to pull back the reins and get involved. **It's time to TAKE CONTROL.**

REWARD

THE FREQUENT FRAUDSTER

★ **REPORT IMMEDIATELY** ★

DATA BREACH LIABILITY
- STEALS CUSTOMER CREDIT CARD INFORMATION
- MANIPULATES TIP AMOUNTS ON CREDIT CARD SLIPS

CHAPTER 8
FREQUENT FRAUDSTER

One of the worst things that can happen to a restaurant in the United States is a data breach. Many restaurant owners believe they are protected if they "dip the chip" instead of swiping the card. But servers, bartenders and even managers who have access to customer credit card information can compromise a restaurant or bar and create a costly data breach *(which can literally put you out of business overnight.)*

In this chapter, we are going to expand on one of the most damaging criminals operating inside of your business: **the Frequent Fraudster.** Unfortunately, even having *just ONE* Frequent Fraudster under your employment can **put you out of business.** We are going to take a deep dive into their various schemes and methods of operation, including the consequences FOR YOU.

Remember, at Jack and Jill's Gastropub when Darren changed the tip amount on the receipt from $40 to $48? Or when Manny used the device in his apron pocket to capture the credit card numbers throughout his shift? Both servers were Frequent Fraudsters. Manny was putting Jack and Jill's Gastropub in tremendous jeopardy with his scam. At some point, every compromised credit card that Manny has stolen will be reported. The compromised cards will all lead back to Jack and Jill's as a "common point of purchase," and it will be determined that a data breach occurred.

This investigation may or may not involve the US Secret Service. If Jack and Jill have ANY violations of PCI compliance, they will probably be on the hook for the breach. Besides thousands of dollars in fines and having to replace every single compromised card at a cost of $3-$10 each[1] - Jack and Jill's reputation will be a total dumpster fire. Nobody wants to eat at a restaurant where credit card numbers get compromised. *News flash: Data breaches are very newsworthy, so good luck keeping it a secret, Jack and Jill.* It is only a matter of time before Manny's Frequent Fraudster bullshit causes a major headache for the Gastropub.

WHAT IF THERE ARE FREQUENT FRAUDSTERS IN YOUR MIDST?

Frequent Fraudsters don't cost you much on the front end. The actual day of their heist won't impact your bottom line at all. But down the road, the Frequent Fraudster creates a chain reaction… a domino effect from hell, all for you.

Chargebacks are a given. They will happen when a Frequent Fraudster has manipulated tips on receipts. A chargeback is not only going to cost you the initial processing fee but also the processing fee to refund. There will be a separate "chargeback fee" assessed and don't forget- you lose all the money for the initial purchase and the tip you paid to the server. When servers are stealing credit card numbers and either using the card numbers for their own purchases or selling the card data, **IT WILL ALL BE TRACKED BACK TO YOU.** And then get ready for all hell to break loose.

The good news is that you can completely shutdown this crook if you will do the work to protect yourself.

THE UNCOMFORTABLE TRUTH

Bank of America / Ziosk commentary (citing IBM) estimated the average cost of a data breach in the hospitality industry between March 2023 and February 2024 at $3.82 million.[2]

$3.82 MILLION DOLLARS!

$3.82 MILLION DOLLARS!!!

Maybe you would be below the average cost if you had a compromise… but odds are that you could also be *ABOVE* average. Like any other gamble, you never know what you're gonna get when your number is up and you are hit with a data breach.

What would it mean if this happened in *your* business? Would you be able to stay open?

Do you have $3.82 million lying around?

NEWSWORTHY

In the past couple of decades, Frequent Fraudster behavior has run rampant throughout the hospitality industry. We had no shortage of newsworthy stories to pick from so we decided to share several different scenarios to showcase the various ways these people operate. Let's dig in:

Washington, DC & Maryland

In 2009, wired.com published this article, "Washington D.C. Restaurants Become Credit Card Cloning Hot Spots." A group of former servers at three upscale Washington D.C, restaurants (blocks from the White House) got arrested for allegedly using covert skimming devices to clone customer credit card data. The heist went on FOR A YEAR and racked up $750,000 in fraudulent charges. The servers worked at Clyde's of Gallery Place, M&S Grill, and 701 Restaurant, along with some Maryland workers at Carrabba's Italian Grill and the Gaylord Hotel.

The Secret Service reported that a 28-year-old Maryland man ended up with the data and was repeatedly caught on surveillance video using the counterfeit cards with the skimmed account numbers. The thief was purchasing American Express gift cards at Target and Walmart stores, then redeeming them at high-end shops like Barney's of New York and Gucci. The servers earned up to $50 per card number stolen. Citibank spotted the D.C. skimming ring when they noticed chunks of fraudulent transactions immediately following legitimate card use at Clyde's (where cards skimmed by a single server wound up accounting for $107,000 in bogus charges.)

The most prestigious hot spot was 701 Restaurant where cash register logs tied $38,000 in fraudulent transactions to cards handled by one specific server. At the request of the Secret Service, the restaurant owner kept the server on for another week while the government firmed up its case. "We watched her very carefully that week," said the owner. "She was the nicest person. I don't know. Maybe this is a sign of the economy. It's very sad when people do these things. I mean, she was making excellent money working at the restaurant. But I guess it's never enough."[3]

Tennessee

Action News 5 Tennessee reported in November 2014 about a skimming incident at McDonald's. The restaurant's former manager and her boyfriend were allegedly co-leaders of an identity theft ring that was running out of the McDonald's franchise. The couple, along with an untold number of accomplices, collected and organized nearly three dozen customers' credit and debit card numbers before they were caught.

Apparently, the victims would order their food, pull up to the window, and then a cashier or someone posing as a cashier would take their cards. Then, the cashier would tell the customers that their orders were delayed and then instruct them to pull up to wait for their food. The customer would pull up, and the cashier would continue to hold on to their cards.

While customers waited for their orders to be delivered and their cards to be returned, someone inside the McDonald's would skim the card data.[4]

Florida

And if one McDonald's story wasn't enough for you, ABC News reported in July 2014 about ANOTHER McDonald's skimming situation. A camera caught an employee at a McDonald's in Boca Raton, Florida, using a handheld skimmer to swipe customer cards.

It was a customer who was auditing his credit card accounts that actually noticed the crime and reported it to local police. The police then checked the franchise location's surveillance footage and, sure enough, the footage showed the drive-thru window attendant swiping the customer's card twice. The first swipe was to charge for an iced tea, but the second swipe was through a skimmer, which was kept out of sight from drivers. Police said that up to 70 different customers had been "skimmed" by the employee.

After pleading guilty to fraud charges, the court sentenced the McDonald's employee to two years' probation.[5]

This Frequent Fraudster got off WAY too easy based on how much damage they did to the business and their customers.

WORD ON THE STREET

For our investigation on Frequent Fraudsters, we reached out to a variety of experts. The information they shared with us was truly shocking. The stories we heard while researching this topic made us *WAY* more aware of who was holding our own credit cards when we were personally dining out. Now, it is a relief to us when pay at the table is available but when the server leaves the table with our card in hand to settle the check, we are uncomfortably aware of the legitimate risk of having our card data stolen. Let's see how *YOU* feel after hearing some of these stories:

Small Bakery Chain in Texas

We met with the owner of a small bakery chain, who had a very dishonest assistant. We share portions of our conversation with this bakery owner in other chapters, but this excerpt is specific to the assistant being a Frequent Fraudster.

> "My assistant was a hard worker. She had a hustle and she could multitask. That was why I loved her, you know? One day, I had a customer who called me saying that she had paid over the phone for something and that her credit card was stolen that night and I was like, there's nobody here that would've done that! Then I had somebody else, like a month later that said the same thing and I was like, I mean, I've got a bunch of high school girls here. Nobody would've done that! Then, come to find out later on, it was my assistant. So humiliating."

If you allow your employees to take payments over the phone, you are giving them access to customer card data. Even the most trusted members of your team are capable of theft. Don't forget it and protect yourself!

U.S. Nationwide Chain

We met with a high-ranking officer who was formerly with a very popular and common restaurant chain. We asked her specifically about credit card fraud and servers stealing credit card information.

> "Credit card skimmers were super common, you know, you put 'em in your pocket."

She continued:

"From an end user's perspective, I much prefer having the handheld device to take the credit card. When you don't have your staff having any control over other people's credit cards, that takes away at least one opportunity. I mean, we were [at] 200,000 employees, 2000 restaurants around the country... it was not shocking when someone was caught with a skimmer."

It surprised us that finding a skimming device would be so common, but our source told us, at one point, 20% of the servers were stealing cards:

"I mean, you could go online and Google credit card skimmers and probably buy one off of Amazon. It would typically be the consumer that would come in one day and had traced it back, and then you'd find a pattern of behavior. Servers would even take pictures on their cell phone of credit card numbers."

Knowing the size of this brand, we were horrified to discover this company had faced such a huge card skimming issue. *Why were we so horrified?* **Because we were dining there! Frequently!** Odds are, you were too. Our source continued:

"The thing that's just rampant that you see, and I see it all the time, is servers adding additional tips. Most people, as you probably know, most consumers, don't check their credit cards all that regularly. So that goes back to the adding of tips. People don't know, did I tip $4? Did I tip $8? Who cares? It's $4, right? But if it's $4 off of a hundred guests a day, that's some nice little pocket change. So the end user doesn't catch that as much."

She went on:

"But it's the stealing of credit card information that takes some time to catch and often the employee, if they're really blatant, they know that it's a month cycle and they know they're gonna get caught. So they work for a month, they quit, and then they go to the next place."

The fact that fudging tip amounts was such an issue for this huge brand implies it is likely an issue for everyone. Big or small. Frequent Fraudster servers are probably making way more money selling your customer's credit card information than they are waiting tables at your restaurant. This means that once they get a taste, it will be hard for them to stop and likely that the instances of theft will only increase.

POS System Provider - Michigan

We met with a point-of-sale consultant from Detroit who worked with bars and restaurants all over Michigan. We asked her if she had ever had a client that was compromised by a data breach or had servers stealing credit card information from the guests. She told us a story that fit well in this chapter, but it also worked for the upcoming chapter on "Shady Customers."

> "One of the sites that we had as a customer really struggled with online ordering theft. You know, online ordering theft is very common, where they do the chargeback for their order, and he had that really bad. My client did hire a person so that essentially, if an online order was placed, he would make them show their card when they came to pick up the order and rerun their card at the restaurant so that he would have the card present charges and there was no chance of a dispute. So he would go in, void the online payment and take payment on site. And unfortunately for him, that employee that he hired to run the cards did steal credit card details. The client caught it after like two times, thankfully. He ended up giving those customers gift cards. I remember he was so pissed about it."

Oh, the irony in this story... Seriously, it's awful. The restaurateur was lucky to have caught the Frequent Fraudster in the early stages of his scheme.

Not everyone is so lucky.

Hospitality Consultant - Florida

Finally, we spoke with a hospitality consultant out of Pensacola Beach. He shared a story with us about a Frequent Fraudster who didn't even realize he was costing the business money. In the mind of the Frequent Fraudster, the restaurant was getting paid, and so it was no harm, no foul. Check out his scam:

> "I had a high-end restaurant client who had a server that was closing out all of his cash tickets from every shift to his own personal credit card so that he could get the rewards for the purchases from the credit card brand. The server didn't really think he was doing anything wrong because the checks were being paid. The restaurant owner eventually noticed that a ton of the guest checks were all being paid by the server and they asked him about it, and the server nonchalantly shared that he was doing it so he could get rewards from his credit card company for the purchases.
>
> The employee had no idea about the cost of processing payments and didn't realize that all of these cash sales that he was closing out to his own credit card were now costing the restaurant an additional 3% or 4% in processing fees. The server was just keeping the cash and paying off his credit card every day and didn't see any problem with his creative, alternative payment system. This scam went on for well over a month before the restaurant caught the issue, and it ended up costing them hundreds of dollars in processing fees when they actually

ran the numbers. They didn't fire the server because they believed he didn't have bad intentions and he wasn't trying to screw them over, so they just chalked it up to a stupid mistake and gave him a slap on the wrist."

The Frequent Fraudster in this story was definitely thinking outside the box and maximizing his opportunities. It just goes to show that not all criminals realize what they are doing is wrong and will find ways to rationalize their behavior. One has to wonder how often this specific activity happens in restaurants.

> **Did you know:** *At this book's time of publication, it actually costs a business* **MORE MONEY** *to process reward credit cards than it does non-reward credit cards.[6] Make no mistake, the card brands are not paying for those rewards. The merchant is. While regulations are coming for card brands and it is possible this may change in the future, it has been this way for* **MANY** *years.*

HOW TO PROTECT YOURSELF- YOUR DEFENSE CHECKLIST

Of all the defense checklists we created for this book, the Frequent Fraudster one was the easiest. If you abide by these rules, you can prevent Frequent Fraudsters from committing crimes inside your business:

- **Surveillance** everywhere will monitor your staff to make sure they aren't taking customer cards away from the tables.
- **Handheld payment devices that require tip entry** prevent the credit card from ever leaving the customer's hand. Make sure you have enough devices so that servers don't have an excuse to take the card to the terminal for payment. This will also prevent

servers from making handwritten tip adjustments on credit card slips.
- **QR codes** on the guest check make it easy to pay the bill from the customer's phone.
- **Ziosk devices** on the table are another way for guests to settle their checks easily.
- **Policies and procedures** that are clearly communicated to your employees around accepting credit card payments are imperative.
   - **Over-the-phone payments** should never be allowed.
   - **Handheld devices** should settle EVERY check without exception.
   - **Bar tabs** are a grey area where fraud can happen. Eliminate the running of bar tabs from your standard operating procedures.

SIGNS OF THE FREQUENT FRAUDSTER

Now, if you're trying to spot a Frequent Fraudster, here are some characteristics that will make them easier to identify:

$ **Frequent Fraudsters** will avoid using handheld devices to settle the check even when they are available, often suggesting that they get "better tips" if they do it at the terminal and leave a receipt for the customer to fill out. They will use other excuses, such as "the handheld devices are difficult to operate" or "handhelds are cumbersome for customers." If you have other servers successfully using the devices, disregard every excuse you are given and take a closer look at the situation.

$ **Frequent Fraudsters** may be in the role of cashier or drive-through attendant.

$ **Frequent Fraudsters** may take orders over the phone.

$ **Frequent Fraudsters** may only work at your organization for a short period.

- **Frequent Fraudsters** often work in teams with one person being a ringleader.
- **Frequent Fraudsters** may have access to your back office point-of-sale or processing data, or may settle your credit card batch or have authorization to make batch adjustments.
- **Frequent Fraudsters** may store guest credit cards in their aprons or pockets, where they could have a skimming device.
- **Frequent Fraudsters** will conceal skimming devices in aprons, pockets, around their ankles, or even embedded in the heels of their shoes.
- **Frequent Fraudsters** may have receipts that appear altered. Check every tip receipt the waitstaff gives you to ensure the numbers seem real and haven't been changed.

FOOD FOR THOUGHT

Earlier in this chapter, we discussed the huge nationwide chain that had a terrible problem with skimming and tip amount manipulation. On the up-side, that well-known brand has implemented the technology in each of its concepts to prevent the credit card from ever leaving the guest's hand. Some of their concepts now use Ziosks on the tables, and their higher-end concepts now have to pay at the table.

What we learned from this hospitality giant is that it is worth the investment in the technology required to prevent your employees from ever getting their hands on guest's credit card information. As long as you continue to allow your servers and bartenders or any members of your staff, for that matter, to have access to credit card data, you are playing Russian roulette with your business.

THE FINAL DISH ON "FREQUENT FRAUDSTERS"

Frequent Fraudsters can be any age, race or gender. They can be the quiet type that doesn't talk, or they could be the friendliest member of your staff. Frequent Fraudsters could earn an impressive wage with you- but it won't matter. For thieves, it is never enough money. A thief will use ANY METHOD AVAILABLE to steal.

Just take control! Eliminate the opportunity for credit card fraud by doing what needs to be done to protect your guests! By doing so, you are protecting yourself from certain doom!

If you read this chapter and you do nothing, but continue to allow your employees to have access to customer credit card information- we can guarantee that you will have a moment in the future where you think back to this book and you wish you had taken action when you had the chance.

Don't be *that person*.

This is an easy crime to prevent!

CHAPTER 9
VILLAINOUS VENDORS

We've covered many types of theft that happen inside the four walls of your business- and even sometimes, the dumpster. Now, we will move to the next level in our "How I Steal From You" journey. It's time to talk about some unexpected thieves that *aren't* your employees but who have access to your product, building, and possibly, your bank account. People you have worked with who are supposed to treat you right but who are in a position to take terrible advantage of you. People who may even enable your employees to steal from you too.

Have you guessed who we are talking about yet? Yep, it's time to talk about **Villainous Vendors**. When we say "Vendors," we mean anyone you pay for supplies or services outside of your direct employees. This category includes the obvious, like your food and liquor vendors, but it also includes everyone from the accountant you trust to the artist that you hire to paint a mural on the wall of your dining room.

While doing our research, we came across multiple stories of theft by accountants, food vendors, construction vendors, leasing vendors and technology vendors. This threat is painful because you hire these people to help you, trusting that they are honest and upfront with you. Some of them are in positions to monitor and prevent theft from your other employees or vendors, and yet they have their own secret schemes going on in the background.

Unfortunately, you leave yourself vulnerable to this threat by giving any of your financial access away to your vendors. What you likely don't realize is that many of these folks have a lot of experience in how to pad their own pockets at your expense with creative billing and kickbacks. For these reasons, we have given the Villainous Vendors their own section in our book. A dubious honor, for sure.

At Jack and Jill's Gastropub, Jack's sister-in-law, the accountant, casually recommended a new credit card processor to Jack over dinner. Jane boasted that her hard work in finding this vendor was going to save Jack and Jill hundreds of dollars a month. Jack trusts his accountant and allows her to sign contracts with vendors without even batting an eye. Meanwhile, we see Jane mentally counting her kickback dollars from the processor and dreaming of a lavish vacation she will take with the stolen money.

While there are no precise statistics on how prevalent this practice is, we learned from our interviews with credit card processors, point-of-sale vendors, and similar service providers that they specifically network and target CPAs to gain hospitality accounts. Some vendors that we met even budget for incentivizing CPAs to sell specific products or services **personally** to their hospitality clients. These vendors pay the accountants signing bonuses for each account or even monthly recurring residuals.

Business Wire published a study in 2024 titled "Vendor Fraud Is a Growing Problem for U.S. Businesses," which reported on the Creditsafe "Battling Vendor Fraud" research. Key findings in the report showed that over half of the businesses in the United States reported being victims of fraud six times or more in the year. Over fifty percent of the respondents in the report admitted to losing **OVER THIRTY PERCENT OF THEIR TOTAL ANNUAL REVENUE TO FRAUDULENT ACTIVITY!** The kicker? The report disclosed that **Fake Vendors and Invoice Fraud** were among the **TOP FRAUD SCHEMES** in both 2023 and 2024.[1] Vendor fraud is trending, apparently.

WHAT IF YOU ARE DOING BUSINESS WITH A VILLAINOUS VENDOR?

Folks, you may never know if you have been taken advantage of by your vendors. Being safe from this villain requires an extremely savvy and involved owner/operator to exercise major awareness and consistency with vendor selections and interactions.

Maintaining financial control of your business is essential. You cannot give away the checkbook and pen to your accountant. You cannot leave vendors alone in your building overnight. You cannot trust "someone else" to read the fine print on your contracts.

To keep yourself safe, be vigilant with your vendors, and you will expose the villains.

THE UNCOMFORTABLE TRUTH

Unfortunately, there are few specific statistics about vendor fraud apart from the study cited above. The best we can do is go back to the Association of Certified Fraud Examiners. In their report, they found that fraud committed by people in accounting departments took a median of $208,000 in their scams.[2] Vendor fraud can be hard to detect because it often requires the Villainous Vendor to either work with another Villainous Vendor or even to work with someone on your staff like a Snake.

We hope to reveal Villainous Vendor scenarios that you have

never heard of before with the goal of creating a new level of awareness for you.

Imagine the damage that a Villainous Vendor could do to *your business!!!*

We uncovered a treasure trove of ways that vendors rip off their hospitality clientele. Here are some of the "basics" to watch for:

- **Shorting-** The vendor delivers less product than invoiced and shares the gain with their accomplices on your payroll.
- **Substituting-** Vendors line their pockets by substituting products of a lower quality at delivery but charge you for the premium stuff. They may keep the difference or share the profit with their inside person who's receiving the products on your behalf.
- **Stealing while on premises-** Service providers who have access to the building, especially off-hours, can steal food, supplies or even cash if they can get to it.
- **Fake invoices-** Charging for goods or services that they never delivered. This is a scheme that we have seen where vendors commonly work with a Snake on the inside of the operation.
- **Kickbacks-** Bribing managers or staff to get more money out of your restaurant. Often, this involves ordering more than necessary, purchasing from a more expensive vendor instead of a competitor, or obligating you to exclusive, long-term contracts.
  - Sometimes this looks like a vendor trying to hit their number for the month, so they will give a kickback to your managers for over-ordering. Your staff may think it's not a problem because the restaurant will use the goods *eventually,* but it can

really mess up your cash flow and increase spoilage.

The most damning cases of Villainous Vendors involved accountants. We discovered it is common practice for CPAs to pocket referral fees and kickbacks from credit card processors, sticking you with inflated rates, less transparent pricing and often locking you into multi-year contracts with early termination fees and/or liquidated damages.

While this practice is technically legal, it is ethically questionable since it can tempt the accountant to push the deals that benefit them, not the deals that are best for you and your restaurant or bar. If you are getting pitched credit card processing, POS systems or any other monthly billed service by your CPA, put on your skeptic hat and make sure that you are seeing competitive quotes that are presented in simple terms. If you get pressured by your accountant towards a specific vendor, you may have a problem that you need to investigate.

We also heard tales of accountants padding your payroll by actually creating "ghost employees" and collecting the paychecks for the imaginary employees themselves. Like the Crooked Clockers, this scheme can be hard to detect without surveillance or a lot of time on-site cross checking time cards with employees working.

We found horror stories of accountants making deposits for their clients and skimming part of the cash deposit before recording the numbers. During one of our interviews, a Detroit restaurateur told us about their CPA "balancing" accounts by writing themselves a check from the business for overages they discovered and then recording the money as going to "payment processing expenses."

In our chapter about Snakes, we discussed a case from 2024 where the Cipriani Restaurant Group in New York accused two executives **and a vendor** of a 10-year fake invoice scheme that cost the company an estimated $3 million![3] The Snakes (company executives) could not have gotten away with their elaborate, long-running scheme without the collaboration of a Villainous Vendor, who created fake, inflated and duplicate invoices.

Buckle up because we have some other instances to share with you where Villainous Vendors played a significant role in theft discovered within bars and restaurants just like yours!

NEWSWORTHY

Some of these stories are absolutely mind-boggling, and it's a miracle the businesses affected could come back from the damage done.

California

> According to CBS News, an accountant from the Pacifica Restaurant was arrested after allegedly embezzling tens of thousands of dollars from the Peninsula Restaurateur. The case came to light after the restaurateur hired the CPA to provide accounting, payroll and tax services for three of their restaurants and discovered discrepancies in the bank accounts. An audit determined the CPA had embezzled more than $55,000 from the restaurant's accounts and had not paid required federal and state payroll taxes. The total mess cost the restaurant more than $60,000.[4] Ouch!

Texas

The US Attorney's Office issued a press release in December 2022 on the justice.gov website reporting an Austin-based CPA managing the books for several restaurants who used a client account to transfer funds into personal accounts and falsified reconciliation entries. They discovered the total theft exceeded $700k!!![5]

South Carolina

In November 2025, a South Carolina bookkeeper was busted for wire fraud and money laundering from her restaurant client. This outside bookkeeper siphoned $318,528 from the restaurant by writing small checks to herself.[6]

California

An accountant for a pizzeria in Benicia, California was arrested on suspicion of embezzling $141K from their unsuspecting client. How did she do it, you ask? By writing checks to herself using company funds. The heist went on for TWO YEARS before the Villainous Vendor was caught![7]

Minnesota

In 2022, a Minnesota bookkeeper was convicted of embezzling more than 700K from a cluster of clients, several of which were restaurants. She generated and submitted requests for false vendor payments and then diverted those payments for her own use and benefit. The bookkeeper also manipulated company payroll information to pay employees that were no longer employed and diverted those payments to her own accounts. Some of the fraud occurred through the manipulation of QuickBooks.[8]

These cases show the truly unbelievable damage a Villainous Vendor can do with big dollar amounts and calculated, criminal methods.

After reading these newsworthy stories, *we have to ask:*

- Does your CPA handle your payroll?
- Do they have access to your bank account?
- Does your accountant have the authority to write checks or make deposits?

If the answer to any of these questions is *"yes,"* then you need to get more involved in your finances and start auditing your accountant!

WORD ON THE STREET

Some interviews we conducted in our research were with hospitality-specific vendors. We are sharing the information we gained to give you new insight into your relationships with your vendors and a peek behind the proverbial curtain.

Indiana

We interviewed a sales rep for a restaurant equipment company about her common practices when working with her clients.

"Usually, when I make a sale to a bar or a restaurant, the equipment that I'm selling is tens of thousands of dollars. My company does not do in-house financing, but we do work with several leasing companies that will finance the equipment for our customers. I love it when my people want to lease because I can work with the leasing company to bump the rates and they pay me a commission for it. I can just tweak the rates a few points with the leasing company and I can make anywhere from $1200 to $1500 bucks for every lease I sign. The kickback that I get from the lease literally doubles my commission on every deal."

Note this practice, because it isn't a "one-off." In fact, our research uncovered that it is significantly more common than you might think for leasing companies to inflate your rates to pay kickbacks to the reps that bring them the deals.

Oklahoma

We interviewed one restaurant owner who was very disappointed to learn that their kitchen manager went on a trip awarded by their food vendor as a "thank you" for ordering certain amounts of specific products:

> "So my kitchen manager asked me for a week off to go on a cruise. I was happy for her and thought it was great that she was taking time off to go do something for herself. Then, come to find out, she "won" the trip from our food rep for ordering a bunch of food! She just assumed the trip was hers and didn't even ask me if I wanted it, didn't even tell me that the vendor gave it to her! I had to find out from another employee. I probably would've given the trip to her (or someone) anyway, but it was a real slap in the face to find out that my vendor had a relationship with my manager and was giving free perks to her instead of me. It's my money and my restaurant."

Be sure to cultivate direct relationships and hold regular meetings with your vendors and let them know that if there are any rewards or incentive programs available, that those have to go to YOU!!! This allows you not only to collect the rewards but also to determine if the reward is worth the amount or types of orders required to earn it.

Dallas

We interviewed a point-of-sale and payment processing sales representative who had an interesting story to share about a five-location barbecue chain:

> "So, I had a POS system placed in every location of this barbecue chain and they were doing insane amounts of business. I wanted to get them to sign up with my payment processing because they were using someone else and I felt like they were vulnerable because they were swiping the cards instead of dipping the chip, basically leaving themselves open to a data breach and fraud.
>
> When I called the owner, he told me to talk to his accountant, put a bid together and work out the details. I got a copy of the prior month's payment processing statement for each location from the accountant and went to prepare my bid. I literally almost fell out of my chair when we ran the numbers because I was able to save this restaurant chain over $100k on their payment processing in a year and still profit $50k myself in annual residuals.
>
> I went back to the accountant, thinking I was a hero, and I explained that I was going to be able to save them over $100,000 on the processing but they didn't care. They wouldn't even budge. Just a big, fat "No." The accountant insisted on staying

with their current processor, didn't even want to talk to me about it and he actually got kind of rude."

She continued...

> "Several years later, the restaurant owner finally decided to move their payment processing over to my company. When he did, he told me they had found out that their accountant was also secretly set up as a payment processor and they had no idea that he was actually the one processing their payments. They thought that their accountant had found a payment processor that was a good company to work with and that they shopped for the best rates, not realizing the guy was literally processing the payments in his own little side hustle, bleeding them every month and making a fortune for himself. We did the math and figured out that the accountant took over half a million in residuals from the restaurant. Crazy nobody went to jail..."

Wow, there is so much to unpack in this story. First, the accountant was putting the business in serious jeopardy by not having compliant processing and leaving them vulnerable to a data breach. *Remember how much data breaches can cost a business from the Frequent Fraudster chapter!*

This CPA set up their own payment processing house to handle the processing for all of their business clients. Bars and restaurants have huge processing volume and could be a literal cash cow for a CPA if they were to price the payments themselves but make it look like they were selecting a processor from the marketplace. All the CPA has to say is that they shopped the rates and found the best company and then they could give the business to themselves. They could also do rate increases whenever they want with no one holding them accountable. It's disgusting.

THE PERPETRATOR'S PERSPECTIVE

Here is a story from our survey. This one stuck out as a particularly Villainous Vendor:

> "My best friend from high school was a waitress at a high-end steakhouse in our small town. Over the Christmas and New Year's break, a few years after we graduated, the steakhouse hired her husband to paint the interior of the restaurant. She called me on New Year's Eve, invited me and my husband to go meet her and her husband up at the restaurant for dinner. We got there and her husband had fired up the grill in the kitchen and was cooking an entire tenderloin for us. That night we ate steaks and drank freely from the bar and no one was the wiser. The place didn't have surveillance and the owners had trusted my friend and her husband with the keys. I guess, looking back on it now, I feel guilty. The restaurant was only open about another year after that so they probably had a lot of people taking advantage of them like my friend and her husband did. We probably shouldn't have eaten that steak..." Amber, Sanger, TX

And the restaurant eventually went out of business, huh? Imagine that!

HOW TO PROTECT YOURSELF- YOUR DEFENSE CHECKLIST

Now that we have sufficiently terrified you, check out this "must have" list of solutions that you can use to guard yourself against Villainous Vendors. Remember, you are not out of line for being a stickler and directly managing your vendor relationships!

- **Ensure separation of duties** for vendor activities such as ordering, checking in inventory, approving invoices and key accounting tasks such as handling money and reconciling bank accounts.
- **Require dual signatures** on checks to prevent unauthorized payments.
- **Reconcile bank statements** yourself so you can quickly detect and investigate any discrepancies.
- **Hire an external auditor yearly.** Not only will this put a second set of eyes on your staff and your accountant, but auditors can also recommend improvements to your internal controls. Remember, 60% of people steal if provided the opportunity. Informing staff of an external audit can be a powerful deterrent.
- **Negotiate rates and contracts** with vendors.
  - **Clearly communicate** and ask the vendor if they are providing kickbacks to your partners, staff or accountant. Require any referral fees, etc. be disclosed in their contract.
  - **Compare multiple offers** and take the time to read the fine print. We know it's mind-numbing, but it can cost you big time if you don't understand everything you are obligating yourself to in vendor agreements. For credit-card processors, pay particular attention to interchange rates, markups and early termination fees.
  - **Hire a merchant advocate** to review your credit card statements so you better understand your current contract. Do not allow your accountant to "pick your processor" based on the promise of savings.
  - **Control the relationship** between your restaurant employees and key vendors. Be regularly involved and ensure that **you are the decision maker**.

SIGNS OF THE VILLAINOUS VENDOR

Watch for these signs with your Vendors. Based on our research, ignoring these warnings could cost you hundreds of thousands of dollars. **Remember that <u>YOU are the Customer</u> and you have a right to ask questions, to check references and to demand accountability from your vendors!**

$ **Villainous Vendors** may display resistance to giving you access to your financial records and their work when you ask for it. Those are **YOUR** books, and there should be full transparency.

$ **Villainous Vendors** may do some of your banking, bill paying or payroll for you. If you find balances that don't match your reports, deep dive immediately.

$ **Villainous Vendors** may have friendships with members of your direct staff. Many internal theft schemes involve a Snake inside and a Villainous Vendor on the outside.

$ **Villainous Vendors** may offer to secure financing for you, encouraging you to avoid getting financed through your bank.

$ **Villainous Vendors** may provide confusing explanations when questioned. Your CPA or bookkeeper is being paid to make things simple for you to understand and follow the money. If you often walk away confused, it may not be you. Their dismissive mumbo jumbo might be their way of trying to throw you off the scent of their scheme.

$ **Villainous Vendors** may tell you, *"let me worry about that"* or *"you don't want to bother yourself with that, I'll handle it."* These statements are HUGE warning signs that your vendor may have something to hide. Look out for "Oh, *I fixed that*" too.

FOOD FOR THOUGHT

Many businesses in the hospitality industry offer referrals to other people for getting them a foot in the door with an owner or an operator of a bar or restaurant. While referrals themselves aren't necessarily an issue, any referral fees or payments should be transparent to all parties involved. Your vendors should always share with you how they found out about you, who introduced them, and if they compensated that person for it. If they don't share this information with you, ask them for it!

We spoke to a credit card processing and point-of-sale rep out of Arkansas and she had this to say:

> "My company pays a referral bonus to anyone that refers a business to me that actually signs up. It's a huge component of how I get new business. I always tell my new clients that we have a referral program that pays a bonus for referrals that turn into new business and that I was actually referred to them by someone else. I always tell the restaurant owner that they also qualify for the referral program and if they refer me to someone else, I would be happy to give them a bonus if the person signs up with me.
>
> Our referral program is a marketing expense and it does not inflate the cost of our goods and services to our clients. Our company found that using a referral program and doing a better job of local networking was more valuable to us than paying for ads or doing direct mail campaigns that may or may not actually work. Our referral program only pays for businesses that we sign up, so we're not just throwing our money away on ad campaigns that could turn up nothing for us."

We support this method of operation and find it refreshing to see a vendor giving full transparency to her clients. Kudos!

THE FINAL DISH ON "VILLAINOUS VENDORS"

Villainous Vendors are out there and it is up to YOU to scare them away from dishonesty by being SUPER involved. Question everything! Negotiate your own contracts and don't leave that up to someone else to handle for you. Lean into the areas of your business that you are intimidated by so that you can overcome your fears and own each responsibility and relationship yourself. Don't delegate any task that could involve your bank account to someone else without ensuring that you have sufficient controls and **YOU** are consistently monitoring their activities..

By asserting yourself when it comes to the people that you do business with, you will feel empowered and in control. **It is worth the time and effort it takes to audit your auditors and show EVERYONE that you are watching EVERYTHING in your business.**

CHAPTER 10
SHADY CUSTOMERS

While perusing a local message board, we found an interesting story. The community was discussing a woman in a wheelchair hitting up all the restaurants along the beach in Florida. Once inside, the woman took photographs and inspected the property for ADA (short for Americans with Disabilities Act) compliance.

ADA compliance for a restaurant means providing equal access to people with disabilities by ensuring physical accessibility and effective communication. This includes having accessible entrances, clear paths of travel, accessible seating and tables, accessible restrooms, and offering menus in alternative formats or providing additional help for visually impaired customers. While it can be tough for small businesses to keep up with the ADA, it's super important that restaurant owners provide this for their customers who need the help and also to protect their businesses from liability.

What caught our eye is that restaurant owners on the local message board were warning each other: this woman would sue them and they'd have no way to fight back. If she found anything that wasn't up to ADA standards, even tiny stuff, she'd sue and usually make a killing. Several contributors to the online thread had already lost lawsuits filed by the woman and wanted others to know she was systematically working her way through the community.

When we read the stories, it seemed like she was using the ADA to make money, not really helping people with disabilities. If she were truly interested in ensuring ADA compliance in her community, she could have shared her findings directly with the owners so they could immediately make changes for the benefit of disabled customers. She could have used local news, message boards or restaurant groups to raise awareness without litigation.

So, we dug deeper and found concerning data. According to a recent article published on www.courtwatch.news, this Shady Customer has filed **350 lawsuits** in Florida over Americans With Disabilities Act violations[1]. **On November 21, she filed eight lawsuits in ONE DAY.** The same person filed one lawsuit against a boutique children's indoor playground (where she visited sans child), another against a Puerto Rican barbecue restaurant, and another against a Japanese bar, all on the same street. She also sued Dunkin' Donuts and then a discount outlet store that same day.

This Shady Customer is one of the most prolific ADA litigators in Florida, according to the article. She has filed 70 lawsuits this year alone accusing businesses of violating the ADA. She files her lawsuits in batches and has been doing this for years.

Taco Shack in New Smyrna Beach has been sued twice, including a 2019 case that ended with a settlement. The restaurant made changes after the lawsuit, including redoing the parking lot and bathrooms, but she returned and sued them again this year. There is an online petition with over 3000 signatures asking the governor of Florida to pay attention to this frivolous and abusive use of ADA lawsuits.

While the terms of the settlements are usually confidential, the article notes that this woman usually sues private businesses and is getting an average settlement of $10,000 per lawsuit. That means she is specifically going after mom-and-pop restaurants. She has even targeted restaurants where she was a regular customer for several years before she sued them.

Like most "Shady Customers," this woman has a motive when she walks in the restaurant's door, and it's all about personal gain. She isn't coming in to enjoy a meal or to visit with friends.

At Jack and Jill's Gastropub, we had some Shady Customers sitting at the table next to Jack and Jill. When Jack heard them complaining to their server, he quickly stepped in and comped their entire meal. He then instructed their server to bring out an assortment of desserts to placate the angry guests.

Jack was basically begging for peace and trying to avoid a nasty online review by offering free treats, which is common practice in many restaurants. Nobody wants a negative Google review to damage their reputation. Nobody wants bad press for their business that could cost them thousands of dollars.

So what can a business owner do to protect themselves from the Shady Customer? It's your word against theirs, right? Maybe not....

WHAT IF THERE ARE SHADY CUSTOMERS DINING IN YOUR RESTAURANT?

We don't have to tell you that these folks are coming into your restaurant. You've met them before. You have probably comped their food hoping that they don't raise a ruckus in front of the rest of your guests. You've given them coupons for their next meal to prevent them from going to the Internet to write scathing reviews. Some of you have even settled with them in court when they've slipped and fallen on your property.

The truth is, most of the time, you are the victim in these

scenarios. People bring objects into your restaurant to implant in their entrées. They complain and show you the objects, whether it's a fingernail or a bug or a hair so they can cheat you out of the cost of the meal, at a minimum. You've also had a guest walk out on their check before. Dine-and-Dashers are the "OG" Shady Customers.

Some businesses are proactive in stopping these crooks. At Outback Steakhouse, the server asks each guest at the table to cut into their steak and make sure it's cooked properly before anyone takes their first bite. This process allows Outback to address any issues with food quality or temperature immediately before the issues turn into a negative online review or an unhappy customer.

But that proactive approach can only take a restaurant so far if the customer in front of them has a shady agenda. Some businesses have surveillance everywhere, including the dining room, to protect themselves from customer complaints that could turn into lawsuits. By having surveillance with audio capabilities, restaurant owners can protect themselves from accusations that are made against their staff.

While this "eye in the sky" approach may seem extreme, after all the conversations we had with industry experts and the horror stories they shared about Shady Customers, we walked away with a firm belief that you need an "over-the-top" surveillance solution for your establishment to fully protect yourself.

It's not optional.

THE UNCOMFORTABLE TRUTH

There are many ways that customers steal from restaurants. We heard many stories of condiments, salt and pepper shakers, ramekins, silverware and logo-branded glasses going missing. The famous dine and dash mentioned above is still alive and well. People refuse to pay for food that they say is bad after they consume almost all of it. Customers use fake coupons or expired promotions to get discounts. Customers charge back their credit card purchases at restaurants and the restaurants have no recourse. Customers complain about their DoorDash orders, and the restaurant has no recourse.

Sometimes, customers complain in order to receive gift cards. Sometimes, they switch receipts with receipts they find on dirty tables, in cashier environments, to pay a lesser amount than their actual bill. Sometimes, they complain because they were offended by a member of your staff, and they love to record the complaint process as an underlying threat to you that the footage may hit the internet and destroy you if you don't "make it right."

Shady Customers who take advantage of wait staff and claim they were offended can be very deliberate in their approach. There is an influencer on a popular social media platform, who visits restaurants and orders extravagant meals while filming their interactions with the server. If they are mis-gendered by the waitstaff, they immediately call over a manager to complain and then they do not have to pay for their meal. EVER.

Given that the customer can deliberately choose to make their appearance confusing and the delicacy of the topic in general, this can be a hard situation to navigate in a way that is respectful to customers but also protects you and your waitstaff. Not only is this person getting free food and social media clout, they're doing terrible brand damage to the restaurants and potentially creating personal backlash for the server when they broadcast the footage of their "experiences."

Being in "the people business" has never been more risky. Many people have resorted to scamming as a form of survival and they justify it because they are struggling financially. News channels frequently show footage of people fearlessly looting department stores all over the globe. People are looting the restaurants too. They have simply found different ways to do it and still fly under the radar. For instance, they come in and dine and pay with their credit cards. Later, they dispute the charges and get their money back. A no-brainer.

Disputing credit card charges is one of the biggest ways that customers steal from restaurants. It is easier to do this with delivery because there is often a third-party involved in facilitating the transaction with the customer.

EM Normandie Business School in France and Azusa Pacific University in California, specifically the Psychology Department, published a joint peer-reviewed US survey of almost two hundred customers who received food by delivery. **46% of the customers admitted that they had committed refund fraud at least once meaning that they had falsely claimed that their order was incorrect or had items missing or damaged when it was actually fine.**[2]

This study was published in 2022. We can only imagine that over the last several years, with an economy that is struggling, those statistics are trending upwards. The painful thing about a chargeback is that not only does the restaurant lose the food, they are also paying processing fees for the original purchase and the chargeback refund. In addition, they usually have to pay an additional, specific chargeback fee from their credit card processor. The restaurant cannot dispute these chargebacks and they are forced to eat the charges.

Imagine the damage that Shady Customers could do to *your* business!!!

In the hospitality business, reputation is everything. Depending on how a Shady Customer chooses to target you, they could do tremendous damage, not only to your pocket book but also to your street cred. News of a bad restaurant experience spreads like a wildfire through communities and can instantly turn people off from even trying your food for the first time.

"*Oh, I heard their food sucks*" or "*so and so went there and saw cockroaches*" can easily spell death for a small brand.

The larger brands have back alley channels and large marketing budgets that allow them to overcome negative chatter but a mom-and-pop brand is extremely vulnerable to the gossip of a poor guest experience. Even if the restaurant is doing everything right, one misstep with a Shady Customer could spell disaster for them.

Awareness is your first step in protecting yourself but your safety requires much more than simply "knowing" about Shady Customers. Processes and procedures must be in place for you to survive this threat. The "*what if they come*" is actually "*when they come*", so be ready!

NEWSWORTHY

We went to the archives to find some newsworthy stories for you about Shady Customers:

North Dakota

> In January of 2025, WAFB reported that a Fargo restaurant server caught a customer stealing gratuities that had been left on tables for the waitstaff. The waitress confronted the Shady Customer and filmed the interaction which later went viral on TikTok. According to the article, the man gave back some of the money in question after being confronted, but not all of it.[3]

Yes! Customers will steal tips off of tables if they think they can get away with it!

Texas

A San Antonio restaurant, El Pacifico Eivo, caught a customer doing a dine and dash, according to an article posted on mysanantonio.com in March of 2025. The restaurant posted the surveillance footage of the theft on Facebook The same article stated that in the same month, Hot Joy, another San Antonio restaurant, put two customers in the hot seat after they walked out on paying for their meals. The Asian fusion restaurant posted screenshots of security footage that showed the faces of the alleged dashers on the internet.[4]

As of the publication of the article, none of the Shady Customers had been arrested but the restaurants were counting on internet sleuths to do the detective work for them to bring the crooks to justice. Dining and dashing is illegal in the state of Texas and under Texas Penal Code, the behavior is categorized as "theft of service."

England

In June of 2025, thetimes.com published a story of a restaurant customer lawsuit that is a classic Shady Customer story! The restaurant in question was sued for 100,000 pounds after a customer claimed to have slipped on a "runaway truffle."

The 62-year-old woman who filed the lawsuit claimed that she twisted her ankle and broke her right wrist after falling at Chapter One, a Michelin Guide-listed restaurant. The diner stated she stood to adjust her dress and then slipped on a caramel-filled chocolate truffle which had been "dropped but not retrieved" by a waiter. Lawyers for the restaurant did not dispute that a truffle was dropped, but said that the woman had not actually stepped on it.

In his ruling, the Judge noted during the incident it was assumed that the woman had slipped on the truffle as it was found on the floor and chocolate remains were also on the sole of her shoe. However, review of the restaurant's surveillance footage showed that there had been no point where the woman stood on the truffle. The restaurant argued that the woman had fallen after her right ankle "inverted" and she tripped, and that the "runaway truffle" had nothing to do with her fall.

Several possibilities were suggested for the woman's loss of balance, including the fact that she had consumed up to three glasses of wine, a "somewhat slippery floor," fatigue and wearing high heels "no matter how experienced the wearer."

In the end, the judge ruled that the surveillance video did not show any contact between the woman's foot and the truffle. He explained that the sticky candy likely came to be on the sole of her shoe "after the accident and before her shoes were removed."[5]

This story is a prime example of why surveillance is not optional if you intend to protect yourself from Shady Customers.

Side note- we one day aspire to visit this restaurant and partake in their truffle offering. While writing this segment, we couldn't help but think about the caramel-filled, chocolate truffles melting in our mouths while we smiled big, chocolaty grins and basked in the wonder of a good dessert.

WORD ON THE STREET

Next, we reached out to some Hospitality Owners and Managers to get their feedback on Shady Customers. Check out some excerpts from our conversations and take away some solutions that you can implement in your own operations:

Georgia

We met with a gentleman who owns a small chain of five restaurants in Georgia. We asked him if he had ever dealt with any situations where he caught customers trying to steal from him or take advantage of him. This man's story was very insightful:

> "With every location, I've got surveillance on the parking lot, dumpster, and every corner of the restaurant. It's the only way to protect yourself against lawsuits from customers.
>
> During a storm one time, the local town pastor was in his car in the parking lot at my restaurant. There was a huge storm blowing through and the pastor's car was hit by a flying object. The pastor suggested that the flying object was an umbrella from my property, but it was really signage from my neighbors restaurant. The pastor filed a lawsuit against my business for damages on his vehicle, but the surveillance was able to prove that I didn't have any responsibility for the damage."

Nobody would have ever questioned the word of a pastor. If it weren't for adequate surveillance, this savvy business owner would have been on the hook for the damage. This story is one of many that proved to us how important surveillance is, not only inside the building, but also covering the entire property.

California

Once upon a time, there was a bowl of chili, and that bowl of chili had a severed finger in it. We spoke with the former director of operations for the famous Wendy's finger-in-the-chili debacle:

> "I was actually the former director of operations for the Wendy's franchise that had the finger in the chili. It was in Morgan Hill, California and the customer went into this restaurant and they planted the finger and then said that they found it in the chili. They called a news station and the news station came out and filmed their broadcast, onsite.
>
> It immediately shut the restaurant down. The customer had actually gotten the finger from her husband who got it from a friend. She cooked it at home and then brought it into the restaurant and planted it. I mean, our sales were down 30% in our area. Wendy's overall sales declined like 10% for about 30 to 45 days 'til we could rectify what had actually happened.
>
> But the damage had already kind of been done. The story of a finger in the chili dominated the news cycle for however long, and then, when they found out the truth that it was a customer plant, it maybe made the news for a day. There are probably still people out there that heard the story and think that Wendy's served a severed finger in their chili, and they never heard the truth that it was a customer that cooked the finger, brought it in and planted it."

This story fascinated us. The Shady Customer was so cunning that she *cooked the finger* before she brought it in (*to make sure that it looked like it had been slow cooked in the chili.*) Yes, **hearing this story literally made us throw up in our own mouths**, but what was equally sickening was the financial damage done to the Wendy's franchise owner.

According to NBC News Bay Area, Wendy's lost **21 MILLION** in revenue. Ultimately, the Shady Customer was ordered to pay $21 million in restitution to Wendy's International and the franchise owner, JEM Management.[6] Unfortunately, it will be a very cold day in hell when the crook coughs up the $21 million that they owe. So, the lesson here is that even when you win a lawsuit against a Shady Customer, it can end up meaning very little if they have no assets and the brand damage is already done.

Who the heck passes around severed fingers like trophies to their friends? In what world are people like, "Hey, I found a severed finger. Do you want it?" And then they take the finger home and COOK IT?!?!

What in the actual $@*%!?!?

U.S. Nationwide Chain

Finally, we interviewed a former executive from one of the most well-known restaurant groups in the world. When we asked her if it was common for customers to steal from her company, she chuckled and shared that it was **EXTREMELY common**. Also, because her brand was so huge and not a mom-and-pop, the threat of bad press was a motivator for the company to pay off the Shady Customers to make them go away!

> "I mean, it's disgusting. People would put a bug in their food, you know, and say, "pay me $200 and I won't call Morgan and Morgan."

We clarified our question, "The customers actually blackmailed you?!"

"Oh yeah. All the time, or I want my meal for free, right? Pack it up, I want it for free."

She continued:

"It was also very common for customers to come in and buy a gift card. They would immediately use the gift card and then charge back with their credit card company the actual purchase of the gift card. That happened all the time. Chargebacks happen all the time. People dispute whatever they want. They say, "We were overcharged, we didn't like it" or they say "our food wasn't good" or "we never got our bottle of wine" and the restaurant has to deal with the chargebacks."

In the payment processing world, the terminology for this kind of chargeback is "Friendly Fraud." **Customers committing friendly fraud account for up to 75% of the chargebacks against restaurants.**[7] The hospitality industry is also experiencing a significant rise in "friendly fraud" chargebacks, where a legitimate cardholder disputes a charge by claiming service errors or unauthorized use. **The problem is only getting worse.**

> *Kind of makes you wanna put an ATM in front of the restaurant and tell people you are only accepting cash payments, huh?*

THE PERPETRATOR'S PERSPECTIVE

In our survey, one person said that they had never worked in a restaurant but…they *did* share this heartwarming story about their collection of stolen glassware:

"Whenever my boyfriend and I go to a place that has a glass with a logo, I sneak it in my purse. I have a whole collection of glasses that I've collected over the years, and each one holds a special memory for me. He hates that I steal them but I can't help it. It's kind of like a scrapbooking type thing, I'm just keeping mementos!" Kim, Bentonville, AR

Think about this story when you're ordering dishes or glassware with your logo on it. The "souvenir" mentality is not uncommon amongst your guests. This also suggests that it could be profitable to sell branded souvenirs at your restaurant. But, if you do, keep them locked up or behind the counter!

HOW TO PROTECT YOURSELF- YOUR DEFENSE CHECKLIST

We've talked about several ways that customers will try to steal from you. Now, here is a list of solutions and procedures that we highly recommend you implement immediately. By going the extra mile and checking each of these boxes, you are controlling everything you can to protect your interests. There will always be uncontrollable factors, but the more prepared you are for the threat of Shady Customers, the less damage they can do to you.

- **Surveillance** everywhere is a must-have. You cannot have too many cameras and you need audio as well. Make sure that the data is stored forever and doesn't automatically erase after a short period of time.
- **Hair nets, hats and gloves** in the kitchen are a requirement. Make sure your expo follows this protocol and that any food runners have their hair tied back, preferably in caps.
- **Pest control** is essential in making sure you don't have bugs. One of the most common Shady Customer scams involve bugs in the food and you can be confident when dealing with this situation if you have a solid pest control solution in place.

- **Ask customers** to check the food immediately upon delivery to confirm the steaks are cooked properly and the order is correct.
- **Servers should check back** within a few minutes of each guest trying their food to verify that it tastes good and meets guest expectations.
- **Establish a protocol** for how unhappy guests are handled such as appetizer vouchers, replacement meals, etc and stick to that protocol.
- **Keep an eye** on customers towards the end of the meal, when it is most likely time for them to ditch the bill.
- **Pre-bus** and quickly clear dishes, offering to prepare to-go boxes with fresh sauce sides for the guests to avoid the theft of ramekins and other dishware.
- **Train your staff** to use verbiage like *"thank you, my friend"* or *"no, my friend"* instead of *"thank you, sir"* or *"no, sir"* when engaging with customers. Simply saying *"yes"* or *"no"* or *"ok"* or *"of course"* is better than attaching a gender-defining word. In our research, the misgendering of customers came up quite a bit and we even found a lawsuit where a customer was suing a business for misgendering them. Avoid this mistake by adopting verbiage that doesn't identify a guest's gender.
- **Your Building** should be up to code and have every safety measure in place:
  - **Handicap accessible, compliant** bathrooms should be available for guests.
  - **Rugs** should be in place to prevent slippage and be firmly fixed on the floor to prevent tripping.
  - **Cleanliness** of any areas where guests walk is essential to preventing people from tripping or falling because of debris on the ground.

- **Spot check** your silverware, dishware and glassware to make sure everything is clean for your guests.
- **The parking lot** is a vulnerable place for you as a restaurant owner. Make sure that your parking lot is well lit, safe from any debris that people could trip on, and that any exterior fixtures are properly affixed and do not pose a threat to your customers. Make sure you have cameras watching the entire parking lot.

SIGNS OF THE SHADY CUSTOMER

Now that you have a checklist of things you should implement to protect yourself, it helps to know how to identify potentially Shady Customers.

Remember, not EVERY customer that shows these characteristics is Shady. Some people genuinely have a bad experience. Sometimes your kitchen really does make mistakes and sometimes people are truly clumsy and they slip and fall. It is up to you as the business owner to use these red flags to establish protocols that REDUCE the threat. By knowing how Shady Customers operate, you can be proactive instead of reactive!

💲 **Shady Customers** may complain loudly to attract attention from other guests in order to make you feel uncomfortable so that you will take drastic actions to please them.

💲 **Shady Customers** may seem fine until the end of the meal, and then require that you summon a manager to speak with them.

💲 **Shady Customers** may eat most of their meal before they inform you of a foreign object in their food.

💲 **Shady Customers** may threaten to give you a bad review or go to the news over their experience if you don't compensate them.

$ **Shady Customers** may inadvertently take dish-ware (like ramekins) because they want sauce in their to-go box so offer a fresh sauce instead!

$ **Shady Customers** may film parts of their experience at your restaurant, or take photos of the actual building and surroundings, not just their dinner plates

$ **Shady Customers** may become injured while on your premises. They will likely request Corporate contact information.

$ **Shady Customers** may order extravagant amounts of food if their intention is to charge back the credit card transaction.

$ **Shady Customers** may leave the table one at a time to "go to the bathroom." Most dine-and-dash customers do not want to draw attention to themselves by all walking out at the same time.

FOOD FOR THOUGHT

We spoke with the founder of a small chain of Cajun restaurants from Texas who shared his personal tip for reducing theft of commemorative glassware:

> "The only drinks that come in a glass with a logo on it are drinks that we price higher so that the customer can take the glass home. Everything else is in a plain red cup, except for our signature cocktails which all come in a cup with our logo on it. We price the drinks at 15 or 16 bucks apiece, and the customer gets to keep the glass.
>
> This keeps people from stealing our stuff and at the same time it gives the customers a chance to take a souvenir home, and we charge for it. This has been great for up-selling the bar drinks because we're just using well or call liquor in the drinks that come in these cups, but we can charge more with a fruity mixer

and a dramatic garnish because they get to keep the cup. Everybody wants a souvenir."

A pretty smart way to deal with the situation!!

THE FINAL DISH ON "SHADY CUSTOMERS"

Look, Shady Customers are not a problem that you can simply solve. They are creative and oftentimes; they are desperate. Knowing how Shady Customers operate and being extremely prepared for them is all you can do. Obviously, you're insured for worst-case scenario lawsuits but, if you don't have the technology in place to monitor your operation, you are an easy target for Shady Customers. If you don't have the procedures in place in your kitchen, you can't know with certainty that you're dealing with false complaints when Shady Customers strike.

It is up to YOU to safeguard your business, so don't cut corners. Own it!

CHAPTER 11
OH, THE HUMANITY

You may feel a little dirty and even a lot disgusted with the scams and plots that exist to steal from restaurants and bars. We want to return to our point that while *"only the paranoid survive,"* you can still enjoy the hospitality business.

Gandhi said, ***"You must not lose faith in humanity. Humanity is an ocean; if a few drops of the ocean are dirty, the ocean does not become dirty."***

Obviously, he said this about larger social issues, but it is a good mindset to adopt. You **MUST** protect yourself from theft, but you can assume innocence and the best in people while you do so. As we said in "Setting the Table," put in the controls to prevent and catch theft, and you can keep friendly interactions with family, friends and staff involved in your business.

Besides describing the industry, Dictionary.com defines the term "hospitality" as *"the friendly and generous reception and entertainment of guests, visitors, or strangers."* We know many owners, chefs and managers are in the business because they truly enjoy providing a welcoming environment for customers and staff.

So, after spending the last nine chapters talking about

thieves, threats and controls, this chapter details how to keep a friendly environment while protecting your back.

THE 20, 60, 20 OF HOSPITALITY THEFT

As a refresher, a common saying in the industry is that: **20% of people will always steal from you, 60% will steal if given the opportunity and 20% will never steal from you.** The percentages thrown around by hospitality experts and owners may vary, but the concept remains the same. This gives us a simple framework to talk about how to keep the fun while avoiding the ick when attempting to prevent theft in your business.

THE SERIAL VILLAINS

Let's start with the 20% of people who will always steal. The best way to keep the fun and avoid the ick with these folks is to create as <u>unwelcoming</u> an environment for them as possible. Scare them off, piss them off, whatever it takes to keep them out of your establishment. If they get in, make them turn around and leave!

Your best defense here is vetting everyone you do business with thoroughly, from employees to vendors to partners. We know it's time consuming and you're already busy. But this is one of those situations where a couple of hours spent up front will save money, time and headaches later.

For employees, we recommend a hiring process that includes background checks and, potentially, drug testing. Consider all the stories we've covered and how a background check could have prevented the crimes that happened by flagging a known thief. Even if you just mention background checks in your ad or as part of your first conversation, it will scare away repeat offenders who know they have something to hide or perhaps force them to admit to any skeletons they have in their closets.

We know a lot of restaurants are short-staffed but we believe the adage that *"no help is better than bad help"* and we recommend that you enforce your standards.

For vendors and other associates, it's tempting to use your friends. We do it too! But don't shortcut vetting anyone — from food vendors to CPAs — because of your previous relationships. Also, make sure you adopt the policy that we mentioned in Villainous Vendors that prohibits kickbacks, gifts to staff, etc. This will help the trash take themselves out if they were looking to profit from dirty dealings while working for you.

Last, it may cost you a few bucks but finding an employment lawyer familiar with restaurants in your area to review or provide a simple employee handbook will decrease risk for you and your management team. Think of it as a necessary cost of doing business, like filing taxes. It's worth it. We promise.

It may also be a deterrent if you tell employees and vendors that you will pursue criminal and civil remedies for theft. *You can decide whether you actually prosecute or sue on a case-by-case basis, but putting it out there as a potential consequence from the get-go can cause these serial thieves to go elsewhere.*

THE NEVER-EVER PEEPS

Let's jump to the 20% of people who will never steal from you. **If you find one of these paragons of virtue, treat them like a unicorn with golden confetti streaming out of its ass.** Seriously, make sure you are providing these people with the pay, good working conditions and other incentives that will make them "lifers" in whatever role they have in your business.

Now, you are probably already wondering how you will know if someone is a "Never-Ever." We just spent ten chapters telling you about how people you trust will steal from you. How can you possibly trust anybody?

Sigh, that is the problem. There really isn't a way to know

unless you run them through every opportunity to steal and they don't take it. Obviously, that isn't a realistic approach.

So, our advice here is the same. Put in all the controls to prevent and detect theft. These unicorns won't mind because they have no intention of stealing! In fact, they may welcome the strictness of your procedures because it ensures they won't get accused of something that they didn't do or they won't have to see stuff happening around them that makes them uncomfortable.

For the Never-Ever vendor, it assures them that their proposals will get evaluated based on the benefits they offer to your business, not because of their relationship with the manager. Knowing that they have a fair shot encourages them to bring the best deal they can offer.

THE OTHER 60% - AVOIDING GOOD EMPLOYEES GONE BAD

Throughout the book, we've discussed employees who didn't realize that what they were doing was considered stealing. We've also shown studies that found that stealing is a "contagious" behavior and that new employees that see theft occurring as common practice in your operation may start stealing as well.

At Jack and Jill's Gastropub, whenever the staff showed a *"we take care of each other like family"* culture, it wasn't them taking care of each other but them taking from Jack and Jill to give to another employee. That's not the friendly, supportive environment that any owner wants.

Fortunately, the solution here is the same. Documented processes, relentlessly (***and we mean relentlessly***) enforced.

Look, we know sometimes there're extenuating circumstances that make you want to look the other way. Or maybe you want to be a little more lenient with a star performer. It can make anyone feel like a total a-hole to come down on someone for minor theft when they are otherwise doing a good job or have had something in their personal life that makes you feel like you're kicking them when they are already down.

But you're not being an a-hole. Think of it this way: If you allow theft for any reason, even the well-intentioned ones, you are essentially handing blank checks to your staff, vendors, etc. You have no control over when or how many of those checks are going to be cashed. You would never hand out blank checks so don't give people the same access to your money through theft.

Another very important but often overlooked point is that you are also PROTECTING AND CREATING THE CULTURE of your restaurant or bar.

A popular book on culture says: **"The culture of any organization is shaped by the worst behavior the leader is willing to tolerate."**[1] So, if you tolerate any level of theft, you let that creep into your culture.

Revisiting the statement from a restaurant owner we interviewed highlights the risk of letting that happen. He said:

> "...you can have water for free and water turns to Sprite, and Sprite turns to Coke, and then the owner or the manager's like, well, it's just Coke, and you justify it. And then it just takes an inch. Take an inch, take an inch. A lot of employees will take an inch until you're out of business."

You can think of this gradual increase in theft as "drift". Imagine the course you want to set for your restaurant including your short and long-term goals.

Every time you don't follow your own policies and procedures by looking the other way, rationalizing that the theft is too small to worry about, or whatever, you are allowing your restaurant to drift slightly off-course. Over time, this is how owners and operators find themselves smashed against the rocks as theft spreads and increases.

Relentlessly enforcing your policies is **THAT** important. But, it doesn't have to be all stick and no carrot for your managers and staff.

DO YOU WANT TO PLAY A GAME?

Like, totally a throwback to the '80s but, gamification as an employee-incentive program is very cutting edge! You can include gamification rewards in your employee benefits to keep that 60% engaged and on the straight and narrow. Use your budget to reward winners with bonuses, gift cards, or meals to keep it playful and profitable for you and your team.

Many POS systems and other solutions support gamification, so ask your sales representative what is available. *You should also check with your CPA on limits to this type of employee reward program and tax reporting requirements.*

Here are some ideas on how to bring this management trend to your restaurant:

- **A Guest Experience Scoreboard** for the front of the house that tracks guest feedback.
- **Order Accuracy Olympics** which rewards zero mistakes on orders or bar drinks. Add quick training on ways to improve accuracy to improve the scores.
- **Bartender Speed & Sales** which rewards fast drink preparation based on POS times, upsells, etc.
- **Host with the Most** rewards host staff who meet all targets, such as greeting guests within 30 seconds.
- **Kitchen Efficiency League** for the back-of-the-house using metrics such as ticket open time, waste per station, etc.

- **A Zero Waste Warriors** challenge for employees to think of ways to reduce waste, spoilage and increase reuse. The company can reward this with a portion of the total savings.
- For managers, look at similar games focused on waste reduction or perfect closes that reward achieving targets specific to their role.
- Try a one-game-fits all approach that so you only have to manage one game but can target different areas of the restaurant and focus areas.
  - **Mystery Metrics** is a weekly game where you secretly choose a standard metric to monitor and then reward the best performers at the end of the week.
  - **Team Bingo Cards** that team members use to check off certain behaviors like helping a teammate or selling the dessert special are also a good option. Team members could even enter the cards into a weekly raffle.

A HARD TRUTH

One driver of theft that we haven't specifically addressed yet is substance abuse. In 2015, the US government's Substance Abuse and Mental Health Service Administration released a study on substance abuse by industry. The study found that workers in the accommodations and food services industry (16.9 percent) had the highest rates of past-year substance use disorder. Drugs are a particular problem, with the highest rates of past-month illicit drug use found in the accommodations and food services industry (19.1 percent).[2]

The takeaway here is that you can't ignore substance abuse among your staff, family, friends or partners. Some may think that it's none of their business, but when it can trigger theft and other damaging behaviors, *it very much is your business.*

If an employee has a substance abuse problem, we encourage you to seek industry resources on how to address it. You might also consider how much your staff is spending drinking during or after hours. This could be a source of theft or may be enabling/encouraging their substance abuse.

To provide more support, spend a little time finding local resources that you can offer to your staff on substance abuse, homelessness, mental health and other issues that you know they may encounter. Since many hospitality workers don't have health insurance, they may not know where to turn. Putting resources in the staff breakroom or with your other employment postings can be a discreet way to help.

Finally, you can openly discuss mental health and substance abuse as real issues to reduce the stigma and encourage your staff to come talk to you. While you may still have to let people go, you can still be the compassionate human being that helps them get better.

NEWSWORTHY

In September 2025, CBS News Colorado reported on a Denver restaurant's partnership with local mental health resources. Citing a Culinary Hospitality Outreach Wellness study, which found that 63% of hospitality workers suffer from depression, the article interviewed the COO of a two-restaurant company that employs 135 people.

The COO said it's the most widely used benefit she offers, and many of her employees have taken advantage of the free resources because it's local, easy to access and affordable. She says: "Being able to offer that benefit, that is huge, both in terms of hiring, employee retention and also for my team...people have just been so appreciative of what they get from their therapy sessions."[3]

Your restaurant could offer this benefit by partnering with a local non-profit that offers affordable mental health support for the uninsured and underinsured.

The key lesson is to show that you care in other ways, and before theft happens. This allows you to support your team during the difficulties of life while still holding firm on a zero-tolerance policy on theft.

STAND FIRM BUT KEEP CARING

With any change to your business, you need to start by budgeting how much you can spend on additional employee programs. There are industry resources available that can give you benchmarks to determine where you may be above or below industry averages for your type of restaurant for labor and other costs.

Once you set your budget, start with the obvious: Are your wages, average tips, etc. competitive and keeping up with cost-of-living increases in your area? If not, everyone appreciates a raise, and knowing that you are competitive will help you hold thieves accountable when you do catch them! Knowing you have done everything in your power to provide a good place for people to work will empower you to do what is best for the business when it comes to managing your loss prevention.

If you can't or don't want to lock in higher labor costs through raises, consider a profit-sharing program with your employees. This approach has all kinds of goodness. With employees making more money when the restaurant does, they will have the ownership mentality that you want. **Your staff will start looking for ways to lower costs, upsell and may even be more comfortable telling you about theft that they witness.**

This can also be a chance to educate your staff on what the margins actually are, which can eliminate rationalization about the misconception of the owner making "big bucks" while the employees barely scrape by. We recommend you consult your CPA and/or lawyer if you decide to explore this approach to ensure the numbers work and to detail the program in a formal policy or procedure.

Finally, if you see large discrepancies in how much your servers are getting tipped and you have ruled out the manipulation of credit card receipts as the cause (*like we discussed in Frequent Fraudsters*) get your servers together and have your higher tip earners share their "tricks of the trade" with the team. Since tipping is a good indicator of customer satisfaction, this kind of training will improve both your overall guest experiences AND your server's take-home.

KEEP YOUR FINGER ON THE PULSE OF YOUR TEAM

This is not a one-time exercise. You need to keep up with what's going on with your team and insist that your managers do the same. Changes in people's personal lives bleed over into work and could cause a trusted employee to turn to stealing. Besides addiction, other changes like a partner losing their job, illness in the family, etc., are common events.

The data about hospitality workers needing help at some point in their careers is another heartbreaker. **According to Giving Kitchen, the James Beard Award-winning nonprofit that** provides emergency assistance to hospitality workers, a food service worker reaches out for help every 28 minutes. 71% of those getting financial help said it prevented them from missing meals. Food shortages were hitting not just the workers, but their families too, since there were 1200 kids in the surveyed homes.[4]

Here are some other ideas where you can help with food insecurity and stay within a budget:

- Acknowledge it as an issue so your staff feels more comfortable asking for help. Like addiction, lowering the stigma associated will increase the likelihood that people will come talk to you or a manager about their situation.
- Create a structured "family meal" plan. One meal a shift made from leftover or bulk ingredients that feeds the team and, possibly, allows each team member an extra plate to take home.
- "Take-Home Bag" policy which allows employees to take home pre-approved leftovers, expired-but-safe products, or family-meal portions at closing.
- Emergency Support Fund or "Kindness Kitty" where a small fund or jar is set aside for staff (and management) to contribute to help a coworker in crisis with items such as groceries, bus passes, or bills. Match contributions, if possible.
- Partner with local food banks and meal programs. You can support the charity as a giveback to your community, which gives you free exposure, and it introduces your staff to these local non-profits so they know where to get help.
- Implement "Earned Meal Credits" based on performance metrics such as perfect attendance, upselling, etc. This helps the business and allows your

team to earn what they need in a way that preserves their dignity and your bottom line.
- "Little Free Food Pantry", like the Little Free Library concept, create a small, discreet cabinet with staples where employees can share extra food or take some if needed. The restaurant can periodically stock the pantry with low-cost but nutritious items that will be a lifeline for team members that need it but won't tempt anyone to resell or take advantage of the program. Employees can also contribute to the pantry if they choose to.

Showing you care when things get hard for your staff is good business.

THE WALLS HAVE EYES AND EARS

We've made ourselves hoarse with the number of times that we have recommended surveillance in your restaurant. *We are going to assume that you have already implemented or improved your camera coverage based on earlier chapters.*

There is another way to increase oversight while you are not on-site, and that is to establish a process that allows employees to report anything suspicious or in need of improving.

Here are a few ideas for this type of process:

- Anonymous tip system with an email, hotline, box, etc.
- Zero-retaliation policy to protect whistleblowers
- Reward system to encourage proactive honesty
- Team training on the impact of theft so everyone sees how theft negatively impacts the restaurant and can easily identify when they see colleagues participating in theft

Make sure that your employees feel safe and are rewarded, or these processes will fall short.

It sucks, but many of your employees will feel more disloyal for reporting theft than they will for keeping silent about it. Friendship with the thieves or fear of retaliation can keep them silent. *It's also common for employees to think of the restaurant as a thing, not a person. Because a thing doesn't have feelings that can be hurt, they will protect their buddy instead.*

WHEN ALL ELSE FAILS...

There comes a time when the best solution is letting an employee go. While this seems obvious, our research shows that a lot of owner/operators struggle with this step, especially for petty theft. This "Accountability Dilemma" is not just avoiding the hard conversation; it's the concern that the cost of firing the person, including potential unemployment insurance and wrongful termination costs, outweighs the cost of the theft.

A 2018 settlement proved these concerns are genuine; the settlement involved a former Chipotle manager who was fired for stealing $626 dollars from the safe. When she sued Chipotle for wrongful termination, the surveillance video used to fire her had been deleted, so Chipotle couldn't show the evidence to the court. **This Cash Stasher walked away with a $7.97 MILLION settlement.**[5]

We put this one in the OMFG category.

Hence the dilemma...if thieves go unpunished, you could go out of business but, if they are fired, you could still go out of business. FML.

As we've already advised, you really need to spend some

time and money on an employment or HR lawyer to get a strategy and documentation in place to protect yourself. However, we can offer the following advice from our research as best practices to add to that strategy discussion:

- Put somewhat broad rules in your employee handbook for theft and theft prevention like limiting personal items at work. This will allow you more leeway in addressing issues.
- Have a documented investigation process written or reviewed and approved by an HR attorney or similar expert and follow it <u>every</u> time.
- If possible, give the employee the opportunity to quit rather than being fired and charged with theft. Make sure that how you do this is within the letter of the law, but it may be worth not pursuing criminal charges if they will write and sign a resignation letter that eliminates the risk of unemployment benefits or wrongful termination.

WORD ON THE STREET

We interviewed a former restaurateur who lost several hundred thousand dollars of personal investment when his business closed after experiencing theft. Here was his unexpected story.

> "20 some odd employees that were all caught stealing or…let go for various reasons. Maybe not stealing, maybe drinking on the job, but a lot of it was stealing…I had to pay employment tax for all of those employees as the years went on. If I caught somebody stealing and I let them go.

What really...ended in the demise of the restaurant was that I couldn't afford to pay rent and all of the taxes I was paying for employees that I no longer had, because I caught 'em stealing or whatever I caught 'em doing. I had to pay employee taxes on them. So, you know, I just couldn't afford to stay open anymore."

What a perfect story of the accountability dilemma faced by bar and restaurant owners. So, our final bit of advice is to **become very familiar with the process for filing and contesting unemployment claims in the states where you operate.** Make sure you have a process for responding to those claims and, if you have proof that the claim should not be approved based on eligibility criteria, **FIGHT THAT CLAIM!!!**

HOW DO THESE PEOPLE LIVE WITH THEMSELVES?

Somehow, somewhere, you know you've asked yourself this question when dealing with people- especially if you have dealt with a thief. We are here to tell you that copium is a helluva drug and thieves use it frequently to justify what they are doing.

There have been several studies and even entire books written about this topic, so we will keep it brief: **Many thieves rationalize what they are doing so that they don't feel like they are bad people, unethical or hurting a friend.**

Let's take a quick walk through a *"but I'm still a good person"* thief's mind, shall we?

To be clear, we are not saying the potential causes below justify theft. We are using these examples to explain how people you see as trustworthy *(and may be trustworthy in other parts of their lives)* rationalize stealing from you.

Potential Cause / What They Tell Themselves

Feel undervalued / "They owe me."

Are overworked / "They should pay me more."

Toxic culture / "Everyone is out for themselves."

Poor management / "Why should I follow the rules?"

Inconsistent accountability / "Nobody checks, why not?"

Witnessing others stealing / "Everyone takes stuff, it's no big deal."

Personal financial stress / "I have no choice."

Don't feel like part of the team / "They don't treat me fairly, so I'll take what I deserve."

Minimizing the harm done to the restaurant / "They throw away food all the time."

Self-preservation / "I was starving."

Being unrealistic or not honest with themselves / "I'm just borrowing the money, I'll pay it back later."

You get the picture.

These justifications, along with fear of the consequences, will often lead thieves to deny everything when they get caught. **So, if you are hoping for some closure when you confront** someone you trusted with their underhanded dealings, you are likely to be disappointed. The final takeaway is to give yourself some grace when you find someone you trusted is stealing from you. **Our message to you is that it is extremely difficult to detect betrayal when the person is lying to themselves as well.** Reflect on what you could have done differently to avoid the theft, but don't beat yourself up for having terrible judgement. Instead, use the experience to strengthen your controls and oversight of the business.

CHAPTER 12
LAST CALL

CHAPTER 12

Last Call

We've given you a lot of information to consider in this book. It would be very easy for us to now do a "mic drop" and walk away. But our work is not finished and in fact, it has only just begun. It doesn't matter what country you live in or what your bar or restaurant concept entails, we hope you realize by now that internal theft, as well as external theft, are true threats to your business and to your survival.

Just reading this book is not going to save the day for you.

You are going to have to go the extra mile to educate the people inside of your organization and to establish processes and procedures that can cover your ass. The standards you set moving forward will dictate how easy or how complicated it is for someone to take advantage of you.

Making loss prevention education a standard on-boarding procedure for ALL members of your team is the most affordable way to communicate that you have ZERO-TOLERANCE for theft in your operation. By educating everyone on the threats, you are also educating them on the fact that you are aware of the schemes and that your eyes are open. By providing your team with a thorough loss prevention course, you are arming your honest employees with information that will help them detect loss prevention threats in your absence and you are empowering your business to thrive.

Next, we recommend utilizing a loss prevention auditing solution to tie your surveillance and point of sale together. We conducted extensive interviews with a company that provides this kind of solution and what we were able to learn from these experts is that even with a full-blown loss prevention department auditing your operation, things still get missed. The company that we met with actually uses human auditors to watch the restaurant for you. They conducted a nine week study on a very well known brand across over 100 locations and they were able to uncover THOUSANDS of dollars in Sweetheart behavior that the existing loss prevention team had completely missed. Services like this are only a couple of hundred dollars a month, so the return on investment for your restaurant is tremendous. Remember that even if you have a point of sale and surveillance solution in place, it requires the full-time efforts of someone auditing the data to uncover nefarious behaviors. Having a third-party company manage this ongoing task for you is the most cost effective and thorough way to approach data auditing.

Also, we highly recommend hiring a "merchant advocate" to manage your payment processing for you. Merchant advocates are able to keep your credit card provider in line with fair pricing and because of their extensive knowledge in the payments industry, they are able to call out shady processors on their bullshit. Rates fluctuate and increase. Without a merchant advocate, you are at the mercy of your processor and the fine print. We met with one specific merchant advocate who is saving their clients millions of dollars a month in processing fees, and we were blown away by the services that they offer to protect small businesses. We highly recommend this type of service to our readers.

A good tech stack can go a long way, and if you couple that with strong auditing solutions and over the top surveillance, you will be able to protect yourself without loss prevention becoming a full-time job for you.

Remember that a handbook and clearly defined policies and procedures are a "must have" for your operation. Documenting everything is critical to protecting yourself from unemployment battles.

We are always open to collaboration with industry experts and are extremely open to feedback and dialogue around the subject matter of hospitality loss prevention, so please reach out to us!

Knowledge is power, and we believe that if we all lean on each other, as a collective, we can save numerous businesses from the villains lurking inside the industry.

Readers, it has truly been our honor to be able to share the information inside this book with you. The experience of creating this content for you has been one fueled by passion and an overwhelming desire to do good work in our community and in the world. We hope with everything inside of us that this book has had a positive impact on you and that you

will be able to take away from it something that helps to make you better.

Remember, the world NEEDS restaurants. *We need you.* You are the melting pot of our communities, the backdrop of our fondest memories and the escape from our kitchens! You are the artists that can create something we cannot, and we will forever be grateful to you for the sacrifices that you make and the difficulties that you navigate through in order to continue providing us with unforgettable experiences and amazing parties in our mouths. Please don't ever give up. All of the blood, sweat and tears are worth it for all that you contribute to our society.

Thank you!!!

We love you.

Jauna & Chloe

Website: www.howistealfromyou.com

ACKNOWLEDGMENTS

Thank you to Leonardo David Sanclemente (my heart beating outside of my body) for the love, purpose and inspiration you give to me every single day. Thank you to Adriana Sanclemente for jumping in the moment I called on you and for your love.

Thank you to Steve Pritchard for your belief in me, your patience, your irresistible kisses and for your love and support. Thank you to Mom, Andrew and Suzy Q and Toddleigh for being my cheerleaders along the way. Thank you to Uncle John and Lynne for always cheering me on.

Thank you to my partner, Jauna, for taking a chance on me and for getting on the wild ride and never looking back. Thank you to Tammy, Carissa, Robin, Vicki, Dorothy, Mandy, Diana, Lenny, Mohican, Andrea, Erika and Alexis- for your support, your encouragement and for giving a damn.

Thank you to Al Spicer for the encouragement to birth the baby. Thank you to Marty Travis for your willingness to help. Thank you to Lisa Britten for your truth.

Thank you to the many industry experts who gave interviews and stories to me. Your experiences will help save businesses for many years to come. Thank you to Allart Jensen for your amazing artistic talents. Thank you to John and Kelly. Thank you to Adele Depper and Doug Lufkin for your insights. Thank you to Lori Sandman for your guidance. Thank you to Jim Roddy and Sean Berg for your assistance with final edits.

Thank you to my Foxhole, for the confidence I needed to

make this happen, you know who you are, and for me, it's ride or die, forever.

Finally, thank you to Danny Vaughan for being an amazing father, for teaching me your trade, for never giving up on me and for always being my biggest fan.

🩶 love always, Chloe

This book is the realization of a VERY old goal of becoming a published author. So, big breath, starting from the beginning:

Thanks to my parents and siblings for supporting and encouraging me from my earliest bookworm days through my various professional twists and turns. Thanks to Mrs. Jackie Earnhart, my high school English teacher and one of the best educators I've ever encountered, for her praise and for planting the idea that I had what it takes to be an author.

Thanks to my husband, Scott, for being my rock and biggest fan and to my kids for your support, tolerance and good humor as I embarked on another venture. Thanks to Jen, Susie, Nicole, Page, EJ, Jennifer, Leslie who have encouraged me through countless coffee conversations, wine nights and long trail walks. I also second the thanks that Chloe gave Allart, Erika, Andrea and Alexis.

Finally, thanks to my partner, Chloe Rachel Howard, creative powerhouse and all-around super cool chick for inviting me to join this project and co-create the best professional collaboration that I've had in my career.

Looking forward to all the projects and adventures ahead of us!

Jauna

NOTES

CHAPTER 3 - SETTING THE TABLE

1. https://www.acfe.com/-/media/files/acfe/pdfs/rttn/2024/2024-report-to-the-nations.pdf
2. https://comparecamp.com/employee-theft-statistic)
3. Garber and Walkup, 2004 as cited in https://www.sciencedirect.com/science/article/abs/pii/S0278431916304674
4. https://www.acfe.com/-/media/files/acfe/pdfs/rttn/2024/2024-report-to-the-nations.pdf
5. https://www.calrest.org/labor-employment/employee-theft-why-do-employees-steal
6. https://www.acfe.com/-/media/files/acfe/pdfs/rttn/2024/2024-report-to-the-nations.pdf
7. https://www.acfe.com/-/media/files/acfe/pdfs/rttn/2024/2024-report-to-the-nations.pdf
8. https://olin.washu.edu/about/news-and-media/news/2019/09/olin-research-workplace-theft-is-contagious-and-strategic.php
9. https://olin.washu.edu/about/news-and-media/news/2019/09/olin-research-workplace-theft-is-contagious-and-strategic.php
10. https://www.walb.com/2025/06/13/4-former-employees-sga-restaurant-arrested-tHeft-embezzlement-being-investigated/
11. Levi, Mariana, "Employee Theft on the Grand Strand" (2005). Honors Theses. 242. https://digitalcommons.coastal.edu/honors-theses/242

CHAPTER 4 - CROOKED CLOCKERS

1. https://sdccpa.com/hot-topics/handling-losses-due-to-time-theft/
2. https://financialit.net/blog/fraud/time-card-theft-big-problem-heres-how-stop-it?
3. https://restaurant.org/research-and-media/research/restaurant-economic-insights/analysis-commentary/bottom-line-impact-of-rising-costs-for-restaurants
4. *https://www.wtae.com/article/former-ihop-gm-in-westmoreland-county-accused-of-stealing-thousands-through-fake-employee-scheme/65276308*

5. https://www.businessinsider.com/wendys-pennsylvania-manager-invented-fake-employee-wages-police-lancaster-2023-7
6. https://www.cbsnews.com/pittsburgh/news/ihop-general-manager-theft-westmoreland-county/

CHAPTER 5 - INVENTORY INFILTRATORS

1. https://www.loomis.us/resources/insights/four-strategies-preventing-employee-theft
2. https://olin.washu.edu/about/news-and-media/news/2019/09/olin-research-workplace-theft-is-contagious-and-strategic.php
3. https://www.ktnv.com/news/crime/chef-arrested-for-taking-18k-worth-of-lobster-tails-from-bellagio
4. https://www.belfasttelegraph.co.uk/news/courts/award-winning-chef-fined-after-stealing-800-worth-of-alcohol-and-meat-from-co-down-restaurant/a702808829.html
5. https://www.fox35orlando.com/news/ormond-beach-restaurant-employee-accused-of-stealing-more-than-30k-in-food-and-cash-from-business
6. https://nypost.com/2008/06/17/cook-busted-in-lobster-larceny-at-juniors/
7. https://www.thecaterer.com/indepth/chef-arrested-after-stealing-from-gordon-ramsay
8. https://www.abc.net.au/news/2015-12-09/father-and-son-steal-$41k-worth-of-chicken-wings/7013552
9. https://www.fox13news.com/news/employee-dunedin-restaurant-arrested-stealing-57k-since-2021-pcso-says

CHAPTER 6 - THE SNAKE

1. https://www.foodnetwork.com/shows/mystery-diners/episodes/menu-mayhem
2. https://nypost.com/2024/04/27/us-news/former-cipriani-bosses-got-kickbacks-from-3m-in-fraud-charges-suit/
3. https://www.latimes.com/california/story/2023-12-01/cafe-tropical-owner-sued-by-mother-as-restaurant-closes
4. https://www.acfe.com/-/media/files/acfe/pdfs/rttn/2024/2024-report-to-the-nations.pdf

CHAPTER 7 - CASH STASHER

1. https://ecommons.cornell.edu/server/api/core/bitstreams/a0e22520-1388-48e2-b887-fe25f0a27b3c/content
2. https://olin.washu.edu/about/news-and-media/news/2019/09/olin-research-workplace-theft-is-contagious-and-strategic.php
3. https://www.fox13news.com/news/video-bradenton-oak-stone-general-manager-accused-burglarizing-business
4. https://www.wctv.tv/2025/06/13/four-thomas-county-ihop-employees-charged-with-stealing-money-restaurant/
5. https://www.wbir.com/article/news/crime/man-charged-with-stealing-more-than-27k-from-chuys/51-6c7d8f9e-49e7-4a23-ab28-fdec00733c13
6. https://www.news.com.au/national/nsw-act/courts-law/why-cafe-owners-abducted-exemployee-and-held-him-for-ransom/news-story/48674dd88c2524108f6cf1ee8bfccff3
7. https://www.cbsnews.com/news/former-waitress-sends-1000-and-apology-to-boss-for-stealing-el-charro-cafe-tucson-arizona/

CHAPTER 8 - FREQUENT FRAUDSTER

1. https://www.securitymetrics.com/blog/how-much-does-data-breach-cost-your-organization
2. https://business.bofa.com/en-us/content/restaurant-fraud-prevention.html
3. https://www.wired.com/2009/03/washington/
4. https://www.actionnews5.com/story/27388773/the-investigators-fast-food-fraud/
5. https://abcnews.go.com/US/credit-card-thieves-target-gas-pumps-atms-restaurants/story?id=24624967
6. https://www.swipesum.com/insights/the-true-cost-of-credit-card-processing-in-2025-a-merchants-guide

CHAPTER 9 - VILLAINOUS VENDORS

1. https://www.businesswire.com/news/home/20240905297840/en/Vendor-Fraud-Is-a-Growing-Problem-for-U.S.-Businesses
2. https://www.acfe.com/-/media/files/acfe/pdfs/rttn/2024/2024-report-to-the-nations.pdf
3. https://nypost.com/2024/04/27/us-news/former-cipriani-bosses-got-kickbacks-from-3m-in-fraud-charges-suit/

4. https://www.cbsnews.com/sanfrancisco/news/pacifica-accountant-suspected-of-embezzling-more-than-55k-from-restaurant/
5. https://www.justice.gov/archives/opa/pr/texas-accountant-pleads-guilty-embezzling-funds-employer-and-filing-false-tax-return
6. https://www.thestate.com/news/local/crime/article312873170.html
7. https://www.ktvu.com/news/ex-benicia-pizzeria-bookkeeper-held-embezzlement
8. https://www.justice.gov/usao-mn/pr/kenyon-bookkeeper-convicted-federal-jury-700000-employer-embezzlement-and-tax-fraud

CHAPTER 10 - SHADY CUSTOMERS

1. https://maorhan.github.io/files/Pub17.pdf
2. https://www.wafb.com/2025/01/22/every-dollar-is-big-deal-waitress-confronts-customer-caught-stealing-tips-tables/
3. https://www.mysanantonio.com/food/article/el-pacifico-eivo-dine-dash-san-antontio-20231992.php
4. https://www.thetimes.com/uk/law/article/diner-blamed-runaway-chocolate-truffle-after-restaurant-slip-lcvt5w59d
5. https://www.nbcbayarea.com/news/local/wendys-chili-finger-lady-comes-clean/1884507/
6. https://chargebacks911.com/friendly-fraud/

CHAPTER 11 - OH, THE HUMANITY

1. School Culture Rewired: Toward a More Positive and Productive School for All by Steve Gruenert and Todd Whitaker | Oct 23, 2023
2. https://www.samhsa.gov/data/sites/default/files/report_1959/ShortReport-1959.html
3. https://www.cbsnews.com/colorado/news/denver-restaurant-owner-supports-mental-health-through-local-nonprofit-partnership/
4. https://givingkitchen.org/
5. https://www.foxbusiness.com/features/ex-chipotle-manager-gets-8m-for-wrongful-termination

www.ingramcontent.com/pod-product-compliance
Lightning Source LLC
Chambersburg PA
CBHW020459030426
42337CB00011B/162